OTHER TITLES OF INTEREST FROM ST. LUCIE PRESS

The Costs of Bad Hiring Decisions & How to Avoid Them

The Costs of Bad Hiring Decisions & How to Avoid Them

Carol A. Hacker

S^t_L

St. Lucie Press
Delray Beach, Florida

Phone: (407) 274-9906
Fax: (407) 274-9927

SᴸL
Published by
St. Lucie Press
100 E. Linton Blvd., Suite 403B
Delray Beach, FL 33483

To my dear mother Virginia and to the memory of my beloved father, Joseph. You always told me I could do it!

TABLE OF CONTENTS

PREFACE

"No one succeeds or fails in a vacuum." One of my favorite quotes by the late behavioral psychologist, Dr. Kurt Einstein, offers the truth to managers everywhere. For it's the "vacuum" that we live in that's costing businesses throughout the world millions of dollars every year because of bad hiring decisions. The expenditures are not only dollars and cents, but are emotional as well because it's difficult to manage someone who is a mismatch for the job. A decision to terminate an employee is bound to cause stress. There is a price for every decision. It's not easy to tell someone that he or she no longer has a job, especially when you know or suspect that you are partially at fault for making the wrong decision in the first place. In the business environment, more specifically the hiring arena, your goal is to contain costs and still hire the very best people for your organization.

The hiring manager's failure to thoroughly understand the hiring process is costing businesses money and creating enormous problems, and it will only get worse as competition for the best candidates increases and businesses fight to stay ahead of the game. It may seem like a game, because highly qualified and astutely prepared job seekers compete for attention, job opportunity, and money.

Do you know enough about screening, interviewing and making the final selection to stay out of court? How easily will you be fooled by candidates who will try to trick you into believing that they are perfect for the job, when in reality, hiring them would be a disaster? Maybe you are a manager or supervisor who has the authority and responsibility to make hiring decisions but truly doesn't understand the impact a bad decision will have on your organization. Perhaps that lack of understanding is through no fault of your own. However, lack of awareness is no excuse; ignorance won't stand up in court either. I always start my "How to Hire Top Performers" seminar with the question: "What does it cost when you make a bad hiring decision?" Inevitably, the class generates a list which includes, but is not limited to the following:

- cost of training a replacement

- loss due to inefficiency while the replacement learns the job

- cost of recruitment agency fees

- cost of classified advertising

- cost of travel expenses

- cost of the interviewer's salary and benefits

- cost of potentially losing customers

- cost of aggravation and stress associated with starting over

- cost of lower productivity

- cost of low morale

- cost of a possible unemployment compensation claim

- cost of a potential severance package

- cost of potential lawsuit

The U.S. Department of Labor estimates that the average cost of a bad hiring decision has climbed to a whopping 30% of the first year's potential earnings. Other experts agree but add that is only the case if the bad decision is discovered and corrected during the first six months the new employee is on the job. If the mistake is not recognized until later, it could cost an organization considerably more. Should you unfortunately find yourself in a legal battle, fees escalate quickly. Even an out of court settlement could easily cost over fifty thousand dollars.

In addition, there is always the issue of how the individual who doesn't work out feels. Those responsible for hiring contribute to the success or failure of anyone that's brought into the organization. Inexperienced hiring managers sometimes unintentionally set new employees up for failure because the individuals were never the right fit and the expectations imposed upon them can't be met. Bad hiring decisions are lose-lose situations which can be avoided.

My motivation for writing this book has evolved from my work as a Human Resource consultant and trainer as well as my front line and corporate human resource management experience. In both private industry and government I have witnessed excessive waste associated with bad hiring decisions. Even for the most well-intentioned managers, it can be difficult to manage the costs associated with hiring. Today I work with leaders just like you; managers, supervisors, CEO's, and business owners who are responsible for filling positions from entry to executive level. I understand your frustration and also your desire to make the right choices. I know that decisions of this nature are not always easy. As a novice, I made my share of bad hiring decisions, too.

The best advice that I can share is to urge you to understand the hiring process, develop your skills, and stick with a sound process. Arbitrary hiring decisions are very expensive. Relying too much on gut feelings is dangerous. Not knowing what you're really looking for can bankrupt your budget. Don't get in the habit of accepting what comes along. Short cuts may seem like the easy way out, but bad hiring decisions often turn short cuts into financial disasters.

From deciding what you're looking for in a candidate, to extending a job offer both verbally and in writing, this book is loaded with practical, "hiring friendly" tips for making sound and defensible hiring decisions. Each of this book's five parts concentrates on an important aspect of hiring.

PART 1: Preparing to Search—It's imperative that every hiring manager plan and thoroughly prepare for the job search. Twenty-seven tips in this area provide the basic do's and don'ts for getting off to a good start.

PART 2: Screening—When it comes to screening resumes, cover letters, applications, and candidates themselves, there's no substitute for a thorough understanding of how to weed out the misfits.

xiv THE COSTS OF BAD HIRING DECISIONS AND HOW TO AVOID THEM

PART 3: Interviewing—There is a great deal to learn about interviewing because it's the most important part of the hiring process. By being prepared, you will immediately save time and cut costs associated with poor organization and indecision.

PART 4: References—What if anything, is the value of references? In this section, learn how to approach references and get comfortable with what to ask and how to phrase questions. You will also learn how to get information from employers who are hesitant to talk about former employees because of legal liabilities.

PART 5: Making the Final Decision—Loaded with tips for making the final decision, this section will give you the information you need to make a decision that's right for you, the organization and the candidate.

This publication is designed to provide accurate and authoritative information with regard to the subject matter covered. It is sold with the understanding that neither the publisher nor the author is engaged in rendering legal, accounting, or other professional advice. If legal advice or other expert assistance is required, the services of a qualified professional person should be sought. (From a Declaration of Principles jointly adopted by a Committee of the American Bar Association and a Committee of Publishers and Associations).

In summary, although other books have been written on how to hire, none share the focus of *The Costs of Bad Hiring Decisions and How to Avoid Them.* Many hiring managers are not aware that bad choices are hurting otherwise healthy organizations, making them anorexic with low achievers instead of well-fed top performers. Never lose sight of the fact that your hiring decisions are critical to the growth of your organization, both financially and professionally.

ACKNOWLEDGMENTS

Many people have been involved in the development of this book in one way or another. I would like to thank first, my husband, John M. Hacker, for his support of me as an entrepreneur and second, Maggie and Nicky for their unconditional love during the long hours it took to write this book.

Three people were kind enough to look at the manuscript, which was a huge job, but for which I am most appreciative. They are Angela Bateman, who reviewed the draft with a fine tooth comb and offered many helpful suggestions; Bill Holton, who unselfishly shared his creative genius in critiquing the manuscript; and Rick Rocchetti, a friend and insightful businessman who had many ideas for improvement.

Cher Holton gave her positive energy in encouraging me and was always a beacon in the dark. Dr. David Ryback was a mentor early on in this project. Dr. Gene Griessman shared with me the inside secrets for making it happen. Wally Gardner helped me be in the right place at the right time. Kathie Stebick did a great job of typing the final draft. Family members, friends and clients have cheered me on from start to finish, and for that I am also grateful.

ABOUT THE AUTHOR

Carol A. Hacker is president of Carol A. Hacker & Associates, a leading management consulting firm headquartered in Alpharetta, Georgia, that ranks among the experts in the field of recruiting, retention, and leadership skills development. She is an internationally recognized speaker, trainer, consultant, and author, and for more than two decades has been a significant voice in front-line and corporate human resource management to small businesses as well as Fortune 100 companies. With hands-on experience in managing a wide variety of public, private and nonprofit projects, her client list spans North America and Europe. She is also the author of numerous published articles, as well as the highly acclaimed book, *Hiring Top Performers—350 Great Interview Questions for People Who Need People.* Ms. Hacker earned her B.S. and M.S. with honors from the University of Wisconsin.

For more information, contact Carol A. Hacker & Associates, 209 Cutty Sark Way, Alpharetta, GA 30202; 770-410-0517.

INTRODUCTION

By starting this book, you've just taken the first step toward eliminating bad hiring decisions and the associated astronomical costs. Refer to this book whenever you have questions or doubts and think of it as a quick refresher course when you're getting ready to hire. It's your on-the-shelf consultant and hopefully the end of hiring decisions that can drain the profits, energy and morale from your organization. As a human resource professional, I have interacted with thousands of people over the past 20 years concerning how to make cost-effective hiring decisions. There is little information available on this specific subject; I hope the ideas provided in this book will fill in the gap for you. It's loaded with practical tips for saving time and money while searching for that perfect employee.

The costs of bad hiring decisions continue to escalate. This becomes apparent when you consider what it takes to replace a poor choice, train someone new and deal with a decrease in productivity, lost customers and low morale within the organization. So why not hire right the first time? If the process was easy, you wouldn't be reading this book. In my consulting practice, I've found that no matter how many books have been written and read on the subject of hiring, leaders everywhere continue to make mistakes in their quest for a better understanding of what it takes to avoid making a bad choice.

This guide, which is easy to read, understand and implement, will pay for itself many times as you use the tips that are provided. Becoming a good interviewer is an achievable goal once the process is understood. Resist the urge to give up and simply hire what comes along. Designed as a framework for success, this book will help you polish your skills and make a definite impact on your organization's bottom line.

PART 1

PREPARE TO SEARCH

Businesses operate on money and people. But if you are like thousands of other managers, you never have sufficient money in the budget, and you spend too much energy "fighting fires" and feeling as though you do not have enough time and resources to do a thorough job of screening, interviewing and selecting new employees. Sometimes it's easier to "wing it" or settle for second best just to get the job done. On the other hand, it's not uncommon for those with hiring responsibilities to be short on skills in this area. In addition, many changes have taken place requiring personnel selection and hiring to be the subject of rules, regulations, human values and market conditions that did not exist a few years ago. Hiring the right people is one of management's most important jobs, and it can be tough even for the most seasoned pros. Sometimes on the surface it seems easier to take the hit-or-miss approach.

The population is aging, and labor pools are shrinking. Competition for good people has become increasingly keener. More women and minorities are employed than ever before. Studies have shown that as much as 80 percent of all employers say that finding good employees is their number one problem. Businesses can do more than they think to cut the costs of bad hiring decisions, but it will take education and a willingness to change old habits.

It's no secret that hiring costs increase when the same errors are made repeatedly. Although managers should learn from mistakes, unfortunately that's not always the case. With an average entry level wage rate of $6.00 per hour, it will cost your organization an estimated $6,240 for each bad hire at this price who stays with you for 12 months. For technical, professional and managerial positions that pay considerably more, the cost of bad hiring decisions can sneak up on a business and ambush profits, competitiveness and market share. Even if the cost to replace one person is a minimum of $500 for an entry level employee and $1500 for a manager, for a business with 500 employees and 300 percent turnover, the annual cost would be $750,000! As you prepare to hire, the first three things you will want to consider are:

- Cost per hire

- Turnover rate

- Productivity

Take the cost per employee recruited. Typically, you start by purchasing classified advertising. Maybe you enlist an agency's help. It takes time to screen and interview, and time is money. There are additional costs which you will incur associated with your decision, even if it's a good decision. Aside from base pay, you probably offer benefits which can easily exceed 25 percent of the employee's annual compensation.

You also need to consider rate of turnover and your source for new employees. If the source is cost-effective but you have to replace people several times, it's costing you more than if you used a more expensive source (by source, I mean how you recruit and where your candidates come from). Are you using newspaper advertising or relying more on trade journals? Do you contract with agencies or do you solicit employees' referrals? By looking at cost factors, you should be able to determine which sources are most effective.

Productivity is also important. Are you hiring good producers? Are the people you have hired in the past the most productive on your team? Warm bodies may fill a vacancy, but unless they are contributing to the bottom line, they are costing you money. Determining whether or not a candidate will be productive is another issue which will be addressed in PART 3. It's through interviewing that you get a good sense of whether or not the candidate is willing and able to do what it takes to get the job done. Productivity relates not only to ability to perform the job, but to organizational skills and motivation as well.

There are tradeoffs. Considering the variety of jobs in your organization, it becomes apparent that how you staff your business varies with the type of position you are filling. Your success in cutting the costs of bad hiring decisions depends on many variables. Can you afford not to do everything in your power to learn how to hire the right person the first time? Let's get started.

CHAPTER 1

APPROACH VACANCIES CONSERVATIVELY

Many times little attention is paid to the hiring process with so many other tasks to be considered. But this haste can produce endless headaches. Someone hired in a rush to work in customer service may alienate a number of patrons before it's discovered she doesn't get along well with people. A new line manager may slow production because he was hired for a job over his head.
—Robert Wendover
Smart Hiring for your business

A large family-owned business rushed to fill vacancies as if in a race to beat the clock. Their hasty decisions brought more problems than if they had taken their time and took a hard look at whether or not they needed to hire someone immediately, or at all. In several instances, they could have consolidated two positions and saved a considerable amount of money. They realized this when they discovered that their total of six laboratory technicians was one more than they actually needed to maintain the efficiency and quality their customers expected. They learned the hard way that just because there is a vacancy, it doesn't necessarily have to be filled.

Sometimes we don't stop to ask ourselves whether or not we really need to hire someone. A vacancy provides an excellent opportunity to evaluate and even re-design the job function. Filling vacancies is important, but it can be an unnecessary expense if it's an automatic response without reviewing the current situation. If and when you determine you need to fill the position, take some time to prepare. Consider promoting from within, something many hiring managers overlook, maybe intentionally. Your best pool of candidates exists within your own organization. You know what they can and cannot do; they are not strangers to you, nor you to them. There is a lot to be said for giving a current employee the opportunity to move up. It could even prevent a bad hiring decision later.

Take the time to answer the following questions before you make the decision to fill a position:

- Is the job being done in the most effective and efficient manner right now?

- Can the work be re-distributed?

- Can the work or parts of the work be eliminated?

- Can peak workloads be handled by giving opportunities for overtime pay to current employees?

- Are current employees working as efficiently as possible?

- Could a part-time or temporary employee serve as a limited term replacement?

T$P # 1: PROMOTE FROM WITHIN

One of your best employees just resigned. Should you promote from within or hire someone new? Sometimes your answer is obvious. You may be aware of an internal candidate who is prepared to move into the job, or perhaps you know the position requires someone with very specific experience and skills who can only be found outside your organization. Your decision on whether to look to the outside or offer the promotion to a current employee is extremely important and is one you should not take lightly. Your decision can greatly affect the bottom line and affect the way your organization operates as well as how your employees will feel about themselves, their work, the organization, and you.

It's a slap in the face to your current employees when you don't consider them for promotion. There is no better way to build morale, increase productivity, and make the best use of personnel than a practice of promoting from within. Your current employees are a known commodity. You understand both their strengths and their weaknesses.

Hiring strangers adds a big learning curve to everything you do as a manager. You don't know the individual, nor do you have a true sense of their ability to do the job. Even if you believe you have a good understanding of the candidate's skills and experience, there is so much you will have to learn about the individual's work habits, personality, pet peeves, etc., which you already know about your current employees. Failure to consider promoting from within or only giving it "lip service" can be a costly hiring mistake.

I have worked with several organizations who, as a rule, promote from within. One of those companies is an up-scale furniture retailer who believes their employees are their best asset. I can't remember when they have gone to the outside to hire a store manager. They are a people-oriented business and because of their focus on giving their employees the opportunity to be promoted, they have a satisfied work force, and their stores are staffed with customer-oriented sales teams.

There are times when promoting from within will backfire, but if you plan for opportunities you can avoid the following problems:

- Employees who are promoted only because they've worked with the organization a long time.

- Pressure from someone inside the organization to see a favored, but unqualified individual promoted.

- In the case of a supervisory position, a promotion that is based upon skill alone, without consideration of leadership abilities.

- "Popular" people who are promoted because they get along well with people even though they are not necessarily qualified.

T$P # 2: POST JOB OPENINGS

When offering promotional opportunities to your current employees, it's important to post job openings so that everyone in the organization is aware of the opportunities. Obviously, if you have a small staff, openings are no secret, but if you have a larger organization, there should be a system for letting employees know when a position is available. However, be sure you do so in a consistent and fair manner because unless you come across as such, you are probably causing more harm than good.

A current employee who is qualified for the job may even resign if an outsider is hired. While you might be aware of some employees who are interested in making a change, you can't be sure of everyone's aspirations. For that reason, I recommend posting job requirements for all but executive level positions. That way, employees know there is a vacancy or newly created position and what it takes to qualify. The more honest and straightforward you are when recruiting, the better. People always want to know the truth, and the majority would like to be considered for a promotion once in awhile, even if they are not selected. Employees should be given the chance to apply for in-house opportunities whenever possible.

One of my clients does an exceptionally great job in this area, but didn't always. They had never considered posting job openings. When they had an opening and wanted to look at internal candidates first, they hand-picked employees to interview for the position. They had been following this practice for years and had many unhappy people as a result. The problem was easy to fix, and the company was amazed at how quickly and favorably employees responded to a job posting system adopted as company policy.

T$P # 3:   EXPLAIN YOUR REASONS FOR REJECTING INTERNAL CANDIDATES

After you've decided who will be promoted into the position, be prepared to explain to those not selected why someone else was chosen. Without an honest explanation, morale as well as productivity can be affected because employees often slack off when disappointed. Your good intentions can be damaged if you give reason for people to be discouraged. An effective manager will be sure that no one walks away without knowing what they can do to improve their chances for promotion the next time.

When I think about this subject, I am reminded of a company who primarily employs men because of the heavy nature of the work (although I can verify that they do not discriminate against qualified women). They do a reasonably good job of promoting from within, but a lousy job of explaining to employees why they did not get the job or what could be done to improve and be considered in the future. Management's philosophy seems to be "tell it like it is." I have no problem with that, but for a manager to say to someone: "Better luck next time," or "You just don't have what it takes," or "Sorry, but I don't see you ever moving up," can be very discouraging. The words you choose to tell someone they did not get the promotion could be cause for generating low morale if not mutiny. Another issue for this company was that they believed that because their workforce was mostly men, they did not have to be sensitive to how they communicated bad news. They alienated their employees with their "tough" dialogue.

This organization is now taking a new approach and has a career advancement program in place. Employees know where they can move and what steps to take. If an internal promotion is involved, managers have a process they follow in communicating in an encouraging way to those not selected what they can do to be considered in the future. The employees have responded with a new exuberance for the company, their supervisors and their jobs.

You can work towards reducing or even eliminating accusations of prejudice, unfair treatment and insensitivity by communicating the following to internal candidates who were not selected:

- All candidates who were interviewed were qualified.

- Several specific skills were needed to be the best fit for the job.

- The person selected was the closest match.

- These are the things that you can do to prepare for the next opportunity and there will be more opportunities.

- Employees are very important to the organization. The organization needs everyone's help in supporting the individual who got the promotion.

You can only do so much to justify your decision. However, to do nothing is unfair. There will be times when you select the employee that everyone agrees should get the promotion. There will be other times when someone feels you are playing favorites. You may not be able to please everyone, but you owe an explanation to all internal candidates who are not selected.

T$PS TO REMEMBER

1. Don't automatically assume a vacancy must be filled; look at the position and evaluate alternatives to hiring.

2. Look for opportunities to promote from within. It's one of the best ways to get qualified people, and it also boosts morale.

3. Avoid the pitfalls associated with promotion from within. Promoting someone just because they've been with the organization a long time is a mistake.

4. Job openings that are posted give everyone who is qualified a chance to be considered. It's the fairest way to handle internal opportunities.

5. Rejection hurts and can even lead to legal problems. Let current employees who did not get the promotion know why and what they can do to have a better chance for other job openings in the future.

CHAPTER 2

LAY THE FOUNDATION

The related costs of bad hiring decisions are not always direct or budgeted, but nonetheless, drain profits and adversely affect the overall efficiency of the business.

—Jim Ingram
President, Triangle Packaging Specialists, Inc.

The foundation for any good hiring decision is knowing what to look for. All of the experts agree with this statement, yet many hiring managers still struggle with how to determine what kind of candidate will best meet their job requirements. At the initial stage of the hiring process, identify what you need so that the time you spend in the search is focused and cost-effective.

Think of new employees as an investment rather than an expense. With an investment of any kind, we usually take time to carefully examine a decision before it's made. We may even conduct an extensive evaluation or set aside time for research. In most cases, considerable thought goes into any major decision. Preparing to hire someone is not any different.

We're all in pursuit of top performers, but how we go through the recruiting process varies greatly. Some hiring managers dread the responsibility of finding a new employee, and others hastily make decisions that they later regret. The time and energy invested up front will pay off in the end when a bad hiring decision is avoided. "Searching for a needle in a haystack" are the words used by one manager to describe his experience with screening, interviewing and hiring. Unfortunately, he didn't comprehend the process or perhaps was ignorant of the rules of the game. At times, the process may seem like a game as you strategize and plan your moves. In reality it's simply a series of necessary steps you must take in order to recruit the most qualified person for the job.

Chapter 2 offers tips that collectively will save your organization from the financial and emotional headaches of a bad choice. You'll find the suggestions invaluable as you lay the ground work for one of the most important responsibilities you have as a manager.

T$P # 4: IDENTIFY JOB REQUIREMENTS

Identifying job requirements before you begin your search is more than an exercise; it's absolutely crucial to insure you're on the right track. Many organizations fall into the trap of skipping this initial step that ultimately can make a difference between hiring someone who looks good on paper and someone who looks good on paper and can meet your expectations.

A 150 million dollar manufacturing company found themselves in trouble when they decided to place an ad in the newspaper for a sewing room supervisor. They hadn't determined in advance what they truly needed in terms of work experience and skill level. They interviewed everyone who sent a resume. They argued among themselves about whom to hire. They actually flipped a coin to make a decision between two candidates. That bad decision cost them over $100,000. They hired someone who could not do the job as required. They later admitted that they had no idea what type of employee they wanted other than someone who could oversee 50 machine operators. They wasted an enormous amount of time interviewing candidates who were not qualified, and their "$100,000 mistake" quit after 5 months claiming in the exit interview that he was tired of a lack of support from upper management.

This problem could have been avoided with some extra effort up front and an understanding of the value of knowing what they were looking for, which is nothing more than a results-oriented definition of what they required of the candidate in order to be successful in the job.

As you begin to develop job requirements, start by asking yourself some basic questions about skills and experience:

- What specific skills must this person have?

- Would I accept less skill if the individual had "potential" to learn?

- What degree of experience do I require?

- In lieu of experience, will I accept raw talent?

- How do I recognize raw talent?

- How much am I willing to commit in resources to develop talent?

Compatibility is an important criteria which you will also want to consider and can be addressed with the following questions:

- Do I need a specialist or can a generalist handle the job?

- What is my management style and what kind of person best responds to me?

- What is my organization's culture?

- Is my business laissez-fair or highly structured?

- What type of person will be most successful in the position?

You should also take into account the requirements of the job which may include such things as:

Job responsibilities

- Supervision of others

- Customer contact

- Vendor contact

- Public contact

- Safety of others

- Control of confidential information

Skills/knowledge and education

- Specific work experience required

- Specific skills required

- Technical expertise needed

- Expectations of quality and quantity

- Special equipment needed

Environment

- Work location

- Working conditions

- Safety hazards

- Hours

- Travel required

- Noise level

- Pollution

Physical

- Dexterity

- Strength

- Visual/auditory requirements

- Mobility

- Sensitivity to taste and smell

Intellectual

- Amount of supervision required

- Amount and type of judgment required

- Independent action required

- Basic intelligence

Emotional

- Pressure of the job

- Personalities of supervisors, peers and people who work for you

- Variety or monotony of the work

- Job satisfactions

- Relationships with others

- The degree of skills required

Identifying job requirements before beginning your search will help when you later evaluate each candidate's strengths against your needs. As you prepare job requirements, keep in mind that if you are willing to adjust your requirements to meet the qualifications of a candidate, you need to take another look at your requirements. You are probably asking for too much. Hiring managers who are willing to adjust the job requirements to match a job opening to a candidate rather than find the candidate who meets the criteria as defined are taking a risk. Decisions like this often lead to costly mistakes. You might think of it as trying to put a round peg into a square hole. It just doesn't work and never will.

For example, a manager charged with the task of hiring a secretary screened resumes without evaluating the candidates against specific criteria. She finally selected an individual primarily because she spoke Russian, although her language skills had nothing to do with the job requirements. The reasoning behind the decision was that if the candidate could learn to speak the difficult Russian language, she could learn anything else she needed to know on the job. The candidate was hired but failed miserably. She hung on for eight months because the manager didn't know how to tell her that she wasn't right for the job. The new employee needed the income, so she couldn't quit until she found another job. It was an expensive mistake that took its toll on both the manager and the new employee.

T$P # 5: CONDUCT A JOB ANALYSIS

The purpose of the job analysis is to gather information about the responsibilities of the job; it should precede the development of a job description. It never describes the incumbent because the position is what should be defined, not the individual who holds the position for a period of time. Think of the job analysis as the springboard for developing the job description.

A basic job analysis would have helped a small West Coast advertising agency clarify in their own minds what current employees were doing. With that information, a vacancy could have been analyzed and responsibilities changed as necessary to reflect the requirements of the new position. The agency skipped this process and as a result never developed a clear picture of what the job entailed. Their estimated expenses associated with a search for two graphic artists was $28,000. The first person they hired was marginal at best, a big disappointment to everyone. The second individual quit in frustration after two weeks, because he felt he was "over-managed" by a supervisor who did not have an understanding of what he wanted him to accomplish.

To conduct a job analysis, there are several key steps you should take:

• Develop a questionnaire that covers general job duties.

• Observe the incumbent while working.

• Interview the incumbent.

• Have the incumbent keep a diary of tasks performed over a period of several weeks.

You may want to design a job analysis questionnaire or use the one following this tip. You may find a form that will work well for you by talking to people in other organizations. Many people are willing to share or share in trade for something you have developed in exchange for their idea. You may decide to adapt part of a form or combine several to make your own. In any event, you will need a method for collecting and recording information about the job. For an entry level position, a basic form is fine. For senior level positions, you may want to use a more comprehensive document. The form for the entry level position should emphasis job duties, skills, physical demands of the job, and day to day responsibilities. The document for mid-management positions will require information on responsibilities, including supervisory duties, as well as interpersonal contact expected. Senior level positions will cover scope of authority, decision-making responsibilities, external contacts, budget, responsibilities, etc.

Your end result should be a formalized statement of duties, responsibilities, qualifications, and specifications based on the actual requirements for the new position. The job analysis should be completed by the hiring manager or at the very least by someone other than incumbents, who sometimes tend to exaggerate or over inflate their job responsibilities. It's always best to have an objective person conduct the analysis.

SAMPLE JOB ANALYSIS FORM

Date:_____   **Job Title:**_____

Incumbent's Name:_____

Major Job Duties:

_____

_____

_____

_____

_____

What is the most important part of your job?

_____

_____

What is the most difficult part of your job?

_____

_____

What parts of your job do you feel could be eliminated?

_____

_____

What kind of education/training is required to do your job?

_____

_____

Describe the working conditions on the job.

_____

_____

How much supervision does this position require?

_____

_____

What equipment, machines, tools, etc. are necessary to work in this job?

_____

_____

In what ways has your job changed since you were hired?

_____

_____

T$P # 6: DEFINE EXPECTATIONS

The two main reasons why hiring decisions fail are unclear expectations and bad interviews. There is a direct correlation between the success of a new employee and the understanding of what is expected. Too often candidates accept job offers without knowing how they will be evaluated or what is required to be successful. In most cases, this happens because the expectations are not defined or communicated by the hiring manager, and the candidate doesn't know enough to ask about expectations during the interview.

In my hiring seminars, I always include "defining expectations" as part of the process that includes preparing a job description. If the hiring manager doesn't have a good sense of what will be expected of the candidates once they become employed, it's difficult to maximize effectiveness in the interview. When the final candidates are interviewed, share the expectations and discuss them thoroughly. When the candidate joins the organization, expectations should be reviewed again and later integrated into the performance appraisal process with input from the employee.

Many organizations have job descriptions, but they are often out-of-date because there is not enough time to keep them current. I know of several organizations that do not believe in job descriptions. They feel that since job duties change so frequently, it isn't necessary to prepare job descriptions. Unfortunately, in one case that thinking eventually lead them into court when a disgruntled newly hired employee resigned claiming she had no idea what she was supposed to be doing. She further contended that she was disciplined for something she knew nothing about. Although the corporation ultimately won the case, the defense effort was time-consuming and expensive.

The job description should include basic responsibilities as well as specific duties. Each responsibility and duty should begin with an action verb similar to what you might find in an accomplishment statement on a resume. Use short sentences with one idea per sentence. Keep statements simple and straightforward and don't try to include every detail of the job. A job description is meant to be an overview of what is required.

If there are incumbents, be sure to involve them in this process as no one knows the job duties better than someone who performs them on a daily basis. Take into account the incumbent's problems and weaknesses and whether or not the demands of the position are too great or even impossible for one person to achieve. Don't forget that whatever is written must be clear, concise and accurate. Also, remember that jobs change, and job descriptions will need to be updated at least annually and certainly before a job search commences.

Eliminate the confusion and loss of time during the first days with a new employee by preparing a job description now. Carry it one step further and just before extending the job offer, discuss the job duties and responsibilities with the candidate. By doing so, you reduce the risk of finding out after the candidate becomes an employee that he or she is not willing or capable of performing the work as described. It's important to be open and honest about what's required beginning with your initial contact with the candidate. It can help avoid problems later on.

Although no job description is perfect or all-inclusive, it should include the following information, which should come directly from the job analysis:

- Title of position.

- Reporting relationships.

- Summary of position.

- Major job duties.

- Knowledge and level of skill needed.

- Education needed.

- Amount and type of experience needed.

- Working conditions.

- Internal and external contacts required.

This is the core of information that every job description should contain. It's not meant to be all-inclusive but a good summary of what the job requires. A well-written job description is the backbone of the interview process, for it's this information that will help you decide what you value most.

There are a number of benefits that come from preparing a good job description:

• It forces you to summarize duties and responsibilities and identify the breadth of experience needed to perform the job.

• It requires you to decide how the position fits in with the rest of the organization.

• It identifies the parameters of education and experience needed to successfully perform the job.

• It defines internal as well as external relationships.

• It provides both the employee and the supervisor with a clear picture of what is expected.

• It prevents confusion.

It's not always easy to keep job descriptions up-to-date when considering the other demands on your time and the time of the people who report to you. However, you need to establish a system and be sure this important task gets done. Many organizations have resolved this issue by working with employees to keep their job descriptions current. Their company policies state that all job descriptions will be updated every year at the time of the annual performance review. It's the joint responsibility of the supervisor and the employee to see that it's accomplished. The system works because supervisors are evaluated in their own performance reviews on whether or not the job descriptions in their department have been revised to reflect changes in job responsibilities. Two sample job descriptions follow.

SAMPLE JOB DESCRIPTION

Job Title: Safety Coordinator
Department: Operations
Reports to: Plant Manager
Summary of Position: OSHA is a 1970 Federal Law which established minimum standards for safety and the job. Responsibility for compliance is the responsibility of the Safety Coordinator who serves as the Company's expert in the area of health and safety requirements.

Major Job Duties and Responsibilities:

1. Serve as company liaison with governmental agencies.

2. Set up medical examinations for employees required to work with or near health hazards.

3. Provide advice on protective equipment, proper conditions and precautions for handling hazardous materials.

4. Enforce standards through compliance officer inspections with authorization to issue citations for failure to comply.

5. Conduct quarterly inspections of plant facilities and recommend action for correcting health and safety deficiencies.

6. Work with manufacturing facility in resolving any citations issued by local, state and federal inspectors; take steps to solve any problems and avoid future incidents.

7. Oversee the administration of the worker's compensation program, including working with the insurance carrier to cut down on lost employee time and cut back on unjust claims.

8. Provide a method for employees to report directly to OSHA should they see a need to do so.

9. Review reports and recommendations from insurance carriers and provide recommendations for appropriate changes considering cost, benefits, and risks.

10. Train all personnel in safety and accident prevention and on a quarterly basis schedule and oversee fire drills.

11. Maintain up-to-date information on all health and safety standards affecting company personnel and property.

12. Act as a company liaison with the local fire department in coordinating regular inspections for fire hazards, testing and placement of fire extinguishers and other fire prevention measures.

13. Provide orientation for contract employees prior to beginning the job and see to it that contract employees understand and agree to abide by the rules.

SAMPLE JOB DESCRIPTION

Title of Position: Public Relations Manager
Department: Corporate Communications
Reports to: Vice President of Corporate Communications
Summary of Position: Develop, coordinate, direct, and administer policies and procedures for the public relations department. Also, oversee photography and audio-visual support for public relations, internal communications, training, and advertising.
Major Job Duties and Responsibilities:

1. Plan and implement policies and procedures for all areas of corporate public relations. Evaluate existing programs, services, techniques, and procedures and establish methods for installation of new projects.

2. Provide creative support for departmental publications and for all publications that advance the objectives of the organization.

3. Participate in community activities and civic programs as a company representative; participate in professional meetings, conferences and company committees as required.

4. Be available to provide timely attention to legitimate requests for information to the media. Make sure an alternate spokesperson is appointed to back up the Public Relations Manager.

5. Update or revise company brochure and promotional material as requested by Vice President of Corporate Communications.

6. Organize and establish continuing internal communications through the use of bulletin boards, employee publications and committee meetings.

7. Plan and produce 35 MM slides, slide-tape programs, video-tape presentations, photo displays, and photo layouts for publication.

8. Gather and edit information for news releases, the company newspaper and customer monthly newsletter.

9. Provide staff assistance to all production departments concerning technical printing problems.

10. Contact the media when the company has innovative programs, positive developments, employee promotions, personal achievements, retirements, or other good will information.

T$P # 7: DETERMINE COMPENSATION AND BENEFITS

Determine compensation and benefits in advance. If you don't know what you can offer, find out from the human resources department, your supervisor, the owner of the company, or whomever the appropriate contact may be, so that when the question comes up, you will be ready. Most final candidates want to know the details of the benefits package before accepting an offer. Unfortunately, some hiring managers don't feel comfortable explaining the benefits, in some cases because they don't fully understand the benefits themselves, especially the details of health benefits, which can be very confusing. Others have not taken the time to pull together this information so that it can be discussed with the final candidate or candidates.

A lack of understanding of compensation and benefits is inexcusable. It could lead to a candidate agreeing with an offer that is later recognized as unacceptable. The final result can mean the loss of an individual with whom you have spent considerable time and money. Letting a top performer get away is a costly experience that usually can be prevented. You need to know what the job will and should pay, as well as whether or not you have room to negotiate. Hiring managers who enter into the hiring process without a clear understanding of what they can and cannot offer may find themselves in an awkward, if not embarrassing position.

There are several things that must be considered in determining pay level:

- Know what your competitors pay.

- Consider the cost of living in your area.

- Understand supply and demand.

- Think about ways to compensate, other than by money.

- Check a recent salary survey to determine the going rate in your part of the country or community; be sure you know what employees can be expected to earn.

Are you willing to pay extra for more years of experience than you originally wanted for an exceptionally qualified candidate? Are you willing to let your best candidate walk away from your offer over a few hundred dollars? Is your offer within the range that has been established for the position and comparable to what the candidate's new peers are being paid for the same type of work? Answer these questions before you begin the search along with the questions that may come up on the subject of benefits, and you will be ready for the next step in the hiring process.

T$PS TO REMEMBER

1. Know who you're looking for; determine minimum requirements for skills, work experience and education. This information will help you identify what you need in a new employee in order for that person to be successful on the job.

2. Analyze the position with the help of incumbents before developing a job description. The more input you have, the better you will understand what's required.

3. Develop the job description using information from the job analysis. Keep it up-to-date by reviewing it annually during performance reviews.

4. Decide in advance what you expect the candidate to achieve once hired. Expectations should be clear in your mind. Later you can explain expectations to the final candidate before making a job offer.

5. Know what you can offer in the way of compensation and benefits so that you are comfortable in explaining both, and in the case of compensation, negotiate if necessary.

CHAPTER 3

MAKE ADVERTISING WORK

As the saying goes, 'a job worth doing is a job worth doing well.' Recruitment ad campaigns are no exception. Because ads are a fact of recruitment life, the more creative the campaign, whether display ads, posters or direct mailings, the more successful the total effort will be.

—Jennifer Koch
Personnel Journal

Good recruitment advertising practices can bring a company a wealth of qualified candidates; bad advertising can cost money and could mean a bad hiring decision if you don't understand the relationship between good advertising and good candidates. Most organizations turn to advertising of some kind to get the word out that they are hiring, but the method used can greatly increase your cost per hire. Only you can determine whether or not that cost is within your budget. You also need to decide if the advertising you have in mind will generate enough qualified candidates to choose from in order to justify the expense.

Attracting winning employees is critical to hiring the very best people. Investment isn't about who costs the least, a mistake that many organizations make. Nor is it the person with the best qualifications; it's about the individual who meets your requirements and stays with you for the long haul. The approach you take to advertising deserves more than a passing thought because it can make the difference between a bad hiring decision and a quality professional who is committed along with you to helping the business prosper.

The following tips will provide practical information to help you compete head-on with organizations of all sizes in attracting qualified personnel. The ideas set forth will help you personalize your approach to recruitment advertising and consider cost containment while making good choices. From how to capture the reader's attention, to why and how to use advertisement agencies, you will find Chapter 3 loaded with suggestions which should be followed before you spend another dime on recruitment advertisement.

Advertising can be very expensive, especially if you run the same ad week after week and are not successful in selling your target audience on the advantages of working for your organization. Although word of mouth is still the best method of promoting opportunities, there are times when newspaper advertising is very effective. Everyone wants to work for a winner. How you promote that image can be challenging and requires skills in communication and creativity.

T$P # 8: MAKE GOOD ADVERTISING DECISIONS

Advertising can be a waste of money or a wise investment. Dollars spent on costly ads that don't attract the individuals who meet your requirements could better be spent on alternative recruiting methods. Good recruitment advertising will attract qualified candidates. Only you can decide whether or not placing an ad in the newspaper is the best way to recruit the talent you need for the money you spend. Keep in mind that newspapers tend to attract lots of people, many of whom will not be remotely qualified. The potential deluge of resumes the advertisement will trigger provides extra work, which takes additional time. The old adage, "time is money" applies to good hiring practices, too.

A consumer products company relies heavily on advertising not only to attract customers, but to recruit employees at all levels. They've had a lot of experience in this area and have found that advertising for certain positions is more effective than for others. Not surprisingly, they discovered that jobs from entry level through mid-management were best filled by candidates who responded to their eye-catching advertisements. However, for sales positions, they knew they were competing with many other companies for top people. They had to look to sources beyond traditional newspaper advertising to find qualified candidates.

The following checklist of questions will help you as you develop recruitment advertising:

• How much money have you budgeted?

• Where will you advertise? Will you use trade publications, local newspapers, community newspapers, *The Wall Street Journal*, business magazines, etc.?

• If you plan to advertise in the newspaper, will you advertise in the daily or Sunday edition, or both?

• What section of the newspaper or magazine would be most appropriate for your ad? Where will it get the most attention?

• Will you need help in designing the ad and preparing the content? If so, who can best provide assistance?

• What size ad will work the best?

• Will you use a blind ad or an open ad? What are the advantages and disadvantages of each?

• Will you include information on compensation and benefits?

• How many times will the ad run?

T$P # 9: CAPTURE THE CANDIDATES' ATTENTION

How you develop the content of the ad without saying too much but still promoting the opportunity with your organization is important. It requires more than a position description and qualification requirements. You need to sell your organization in an interesting and honest format.

In developing an ad, think about what type of advertisement will best capture the readers' attention. Be creative but professional and promote the good image and reputation of your organization. Stay away from small ads with little detail. The cluttered look is also a turn-off. I've written many advertisements for job openings over the years and have scanned hundreds for comparison and ideas. I'm always amazed by companies that invest money in ads that lack pizazz and power. If this is a weakness you recognize, get help or learn how to develop ads that attract the caliber of people you need.

If you are going to design an ad yourself, there are several things you should consider:

- **Size**—A large ad, rather than a small ad, can make a difference. Your budget may determine the size of your ad.

- **Layout**—Think visually. Will large and bold grab the readers' attention or will bullets and underlining make a better impact?

- **Type**—The type must be easy to read. Don't use more than two fonts, otherwise you detract from the information you are trying to convey.

- **Headline**—It must be strong and does not have to be the title of the position. It should attract attention and include an incentive, if possible, such as: "Relaxed Living in the Sunny South," or "Join the Leader," or "We're Looking for People Who Want to Move Up."

- **Graphics**—Will you use a company logo or other graphics to attract attention to your ad?

- **Overall appearance**—Your ad should be crisp, uncluttered, and answer the reader's question, "What's in it for me?"

Large block advertisements are ideal but expensive. Smaller ads can also be effective and are less costly but may not be seen as easily by your target audience. Your ad must be designed to get results—without results you have wasted your money. Since you are competing with numerous other ads, you will want to provide the reader with some meaningful information about the job and the organization without telling too much. Peaking the interest of the reader enough to get a response is your objective.

Start your ad with an attention-getting job title or headline and include the following information:

- A brief description of the position including primary job duties and responsibilities.

- Qualifications such as type of skills and work experience required.

- Benefits of the job including work environment, rewards for hard work and benefits or incentives.

- A mention of why the job is available. Is it due to expansion or promotion?

- A request for salary requirements even though some candidates will ignore you. Those who respond will provide valuable information that you can use in the preliminary screening process.

T$P # 10: USE ADVERTISING SPACE EFFECTIVELY

You need to get the most from your advertising, but how you accomplish that takes some thought. To save money, some organizations use very small one line ads that may or may not attract attention. Some of the success of a small ad depends on the size of the other ads you are competing with for attention. It is best to spend a little more and get high visibility with the ad than cut costs and have to run an ad five times before getting a good response.

The location of the advertisement in the newspaper has a lot to do with whether or not your audience sees it. For example, if I were looking for a recruiter for the human resource department and rather than running the ad under "human resources," I ran the ad under "recruitment," I would probably not attract the type of candidate I had in mind. I would undoubtedly get responses from "headhunters" and people who work in placement agencies. Actually, I would want to attract people who had experience recruiting for a human resource department in a corporation. The two jobs are different, as is the experience needed for each position.

Consider announcing several openings in one advertisement and in effect splitting the costs between the positions. I frequently do this when recruiting for several positions at the same time. For example, I've used a large block ad in which I listed openings for a customer service representative, a cost accounting clerk and a national accounts manager in the same ad. It saved the company money and attracted the qualified people I wanted because the advertisement was so large that no one could miss it.

Never lose sight of the fact that the purpose of your ad is to attract attention and to get qualified candidates to respond. You don't want to be "penny wise and pound foolish," but you need to give some serious consideration to if and how you will advertise. Although advertising in the newspaper is certainly not the only way to find qualified candidates, it's an avenue many organizations use and find effective. Some companies have been known to take out a full- or half-page ad in their local newspaper. Well designed with the organization's logo and information about the business, it can attract the qualified candidates the organization is seeking.

T$P # 11: KNOW HOW TO USE BLIND AS WELL AS OPEN ADS

Blind ads do not reveal the organization but usually ask that resumes be sent to a post office box. They frequently are used when a company wishes to conceal it's identity because they are looking outside the organization for new people and don't want their current employees to know. Sometimes the organization has a poor reputation in the community, and few people would apply if they recognized the name. Some organizations "test the market" with a blind ad to get a feel for the skill level of candidates that are looking for employment.

Open ads include the name, address and sometimes the telephone number of the organization, which makes it easier for candidates to apply. You must decide which type of ad is best for you. If there is no reason to hide your identity, then an open ad is more appropriate. Some candidates make it their policy never to apply to a blind ad, another reason to be honest in advertising. You may lose good candidates because they don't want to get involved with an organization that conceals its identity or appears to have something to hide. Some job seekers are simply not willing to take the risk that the blind box could be that of their own company.

T$P # 12: DON'T WRITE MISLEADING ADS

Your advertisement is the cover letter and resume of your organization to perspective candidates. Setting a trap in hopes of luring candidates into your organization can be disastrous! You may be successful in hiring them, but bad hiring decisions are often made as a result, and you will bear the cost of those bad decisions. If you claim to have certain benefits and conditions, and they do not exist, you are misleading the candidate and potentially hurting yourself. Don't put anything in your advertising that is not true or borders on a lie. Misrepresenting your organization's culture, benefits package, competitive strength, and strategic direction can lead to trouble with the courts. Candidates who become employees and later find out that the description of the job which was in your advertisement was not accurate, may have reason to sue.

A small company in the Northeast thought that the dangers of writing misleading ads did not apply to them. Their ad for a warehouse worker offered benefits that they did not provide. Their advertisement included the following:

• "You'll get exposure to all facets of our fast-paced business."

• "Unlimited growth potential."

• "Base pay plus a generous bonus."

• "Ten paid holidays."

The company was challenged by the wife of an employee who encouraged her husband to question the benefits described in the ad. The company could not support their statements, as exposure to all facets of the business was driving a forklift around the shop floor; there was no growth potential for an unskilled worker in a 50-person company; he never got a bonus as "promised" in the ad; and the company had only nine paid holidays. The company learned a lesson and never again included anything in their ads that they could not fully provide.

T$P # 13: FIND THE BEST PLACES TO ADVERTISE

If you decide to advertise a vacancy or newly created position, there are many avenues you can take. It's easy to get caught up in quickly turning out an ad just to get something in the newspaper before the week's deadline. Some organizations make poor advertising decisions and spend money on newspaper and professional journal ads that fail to attract the candidates needed; they don't know where their advertising dollars have the biggest payoff.

Whether you advertise in your local newspaper, *The Wall Street Journal,* a trade publication, or someplace in between, it's an expense for which you need to plan. For professional level positions, one ad in *The Wall Street Journal* can generate up to 2,000 responses. With most ads of this kind, many people will apply who are not a match; they simply apply for everything that sounds good. Trade publications and professional journals can be an excellent resource but in most cases, they are only published monthly or sometimes quarterly. If you need an immediate response, you may not be able to wait for your advertisement to appear.

You will need to promote opportunity with your organization in publications that are available in the communities where people live who would be likely to supply your labor pool. This is especially true for entry level and lower paying positions. Advertising for minimum wage positions in a community where the annual median income is $60,000 is a waste of your advertising dollars. With a little thought and research, you should be able to locate the most effective places to advertise.

T$P # 14: CONSIDER AREAS OF HIGH UNEMPLOYMENT

Advertising in areas of high or steady employment may not get you the candidates you need. Often, individuals who would be a perfect fit for you are not looking for a job and certainly are not reading the want ads. Businesses who look outside their community for qualified individuals often find a gold mine of qualified people.

There are always parts of the country where unemployment is high and job seekers are abundant. Many people are willing to move for the "right" opportunity, even if it means paying their own relocation expenses. Don't overlook this pool of potential candidates. You can find out where unemployment is highest by contacting your local U.S. Department of Labor office. If they do not have the information you need, they will know where you can get it.

When speaking at an international conference in the hospitality industry, I met many creative owners and managers who shared their strategies for recruiting candidates for hard-to-fill positions. Advertising in areas of high unemployment was successful for them, even if it lead to providing shuttle buses to take employees to and from work. They found people were more mobile than they originally thought. Many companies work hard at presenting a great image not only to their customers, but also to their prospective as well as current employees. The goal is to treat every person who comes through the door as their best customer, including candidates.

T$P # 15: AVOID DISCRIMINATORY ADVERTISEMENTS

Wording in an advertisement that suggests discrimination is fortunately becoming less of a problem due to increased awareness. However, I still occasionally see help-wanted ads that border on "unacceptable" due to poor choice of language. The Age Discrimination in Employment Act (ADEA) makes it unlawful for an employer to use employment advertising that discriminates against people 40 years of age or older, as well as advertisements that implicitly discourage older people from applying.

An advertisement can be discriminatory by defining qualifications of education that are appropriate for a young candidate but irrelevant for someone with 25 years of work experience. For example, using descriptions such as "junior account rep," "athletically inclined," or "great first job" are unacceptable.

To avoid discriminatory ads, do not use the following phrases. Also be aware that these examples are not all-inclusive but represent only a sample of what to avoid:

- "Wanted: attractive front office secretary."

- "Only those under 40 need apply."

- "Needed: recent college graduate."

- "Hiring young, energetic people."

- "Youthful appearance, a plus."

- "Growing organization has opening for accountant with no more than 3 years of accounting experience."

Many employers do not seem to be aware that language such as this is unacceptable because it implies discrimination. Most of the violations of discrimination in recruitment advertisement fall into the categories of age, gender and national origin. Discrimination against gender includes both females and males and also involves the way in which job titles are described. For example, the word "stewardess" is no longer used in the airline industry. It has been changed to "flight attendant." "Waitress" or "waiter" has been changed to "wait staff" or "server," and "draftsman" to "drafter." The old term "Gal Friday" went out with the hoola hoop.

It's also against the law to discriminate on the basis of national origin, including illegal aliens. Your advertisement may not mention physical appearance as a criteria for hiring, such as: "we are looking for an all-American girl to join our sales team." The violation here is two-fold, in that national origin is mentioned as well as gender. If you have specific questions regarding appropriate language or how employment laws apply to your organization, contact your local Equal Employment Opportunity Commission office.

T$P # 16: USE AN EQUAL EMPLOYMENT STATEMENT

It's a good idea to include at the bottom of each advertisement "EEO Employer" (Equal Employment Opportunity Employer), which tells the reader that you hire without discrimination based on age, gender, race, national origin, religion, handicap, or veteran status. It's important, however, that you live up to everything in the advertisement including your claim of being an Equal Opportunity Employer. Some organizations include the initials "EEO/M,F,H,V" with each ad and also use it on all promotional literature. If your organization does not honestly practice EEO recruiting, don't include an equal employment statement, as it could be a costly liability for you later.

A large employer in the Midwest misrepresented themselves when they included the EEO statement but were clearly discriminatory in their hiring practices. It didn't take long for the public to catch on, and eventually there was a class-action lawsuit by a number of applicants who charged that they had been discriminated against because of their race. The case was settled out of court for an undisclosed amount of money. The point is, in all of your hiring efforts, don't do anything that would suggest that you discriminate.

T$P # 17: CONSIDER RECRUITMENT ADVERTISING AGENCIES

Good recruitment advertising agencies can be a valuable resource because they can help you prepare and place an effective ad. Some companies know this resource is available but have never bothered to check into what recruitment agencies can offer at little or no cost.

If you're looking for a distinctive, eye-catching advertisement, consider using an agency. Most agencies of this type do not charge a fee but are paid by commission from the newspapers. Many employers are not even aware that this service is available. Your local newspaper should know which agencies are in your community. I can think of nothing more cost-effective than using a recruitment advertising agency to design an ad that will grab the attention of your target audience. I have used them for years and recommend that my clients also consider them. Why spend your valuable time designing advertising when someone else can do it for you, do it better, and it costs you little or nothing?

T$PS TO REMEMBER

1. Plan for advertising expenditures by deciding where you will get the most for your money. Newspaper advertising is considered first by many companies, but it may not be the best avenue for you.

2. Use blind ads with caution, as you may lose good candidates who are reluctant to send a resume to an unknown source.

3. Avoid writing that could potentially lead to a lawsuit.

4. Find out where your advertising is most effective. Newspapers and magazines are a good place to start but are not the only avenue.

5. Don't overlook the potential pool of candidates who live in areas of high unemployment.

6. Never use wording in your advertisements that suggests that you discriminate in your hiring practices. Once it's in writing, you could be inviting trouble.

7. Promote the fact that you are an equal opportunity employer by including an equal opportunity employment statement in your ad.

8. Attractive ads get attention. If you need help, work with a recruitment advertising agency for little or no cost.

CHAPTER 4

STRETCH BEYOND TRADITIONAL ADVERTISING

> A bad hiring decision is an exasperating problem that raises costs, lowers productivity, and dampens morale. Often a hidden expense that may be difficult to isolate and quantify, it is nevertheless a very real human resource problem.
>
> —Norma Petway Cogburn
> Human Resource Representative
> Glaxo Wellcome, Inc.

Newspaper ads may be the first thing you think of to fill a job vacancy, but it is only one of many methods available to find qualified people. There was a time when employers relied almost exclusively on newspaper advertising for recruiting. However, times are changing, and businesses have begun to recognize the value of networking and employee referrals to find good candidates. It may take some extra effort, but don't be afraid to get creative in your search. Creative recruiting involves considering contacts through these sources:

- Networking.

- Advertising agencies.

- The competition.

- Customers and vendors.

- Internally within your organization.

- Professional recruiters.

- Classified advertising.

Good candidates are often not seeking other employment, which means they are not looking for you; you must find them. There are so many interesting ways to attract good people, ranging from campus recruiting to celebrity-hosted events. Of course, everything has a price, and only you can decide how much you are willing to spend to get the right person for the job.

I enjoy the fun that goes with unusual methods of recruiting and am always looking for interesting ideas to pass along to my clients. Not too long ago, I read about a company in the Southwest who sponsored a mini hot air balloon festival that was really a job fair. The employer was trying to attract entry through mid-management level candidates to the hospitality industry, specifically their chain of hotels and restaurants. Their theme, "The Sky's the Limit," was backed by a half-a-dozen multi-colored balloons that took candidates and their families for a breathtaking view of the dessert and surrounding area. Upon landing, they were given applications for employment, and appointments for interviews were arranged for those who were interested. They were more successful than they had hoped and have plans to repeat their creative promotion.

Whether you attract good people in an unconventional manner or stick to a more traditional method, there are lots of individuals who may be a perfect match for your organization. You just have to find a way to reach them. How you do that could make the difference between accepting whomever comes along and finding the perfect fit. I have included a list of creative recruiting strategies as part of this chapter because even if you don't use one of them, you may come up with ideas of your own after reading the list.

T$P # 18: GET CREATIVE

A "Help Wanted" sign is in the window, but does it get the help needed? In today's competitive work environment, employers must be on their toes and open to recruiting in a variety of ways. From the potential to try out employees risk-free for several months to money paid to you for hiring someone, there are many ways to find good people.

Some of the methods used by my clients, as well as other organizations across the country, include:

- **"Welcome wagon" or newcomers' organizations.** People moving into a community may be looking for employment opportunities, and you can find and attract these new arrivals by developing a relationship with any of the newcomers' organizations or welcome wagon associations in your area.

- **Radio advertisement.** A great way to reinforce print advertising, radio can be a very effective method of promoting job openings, as well as be cost-effective if you can reach a large audience or if it's done as a public service announcement.

- **Television advertisement.** It's expensive but can work well if you advertise when your target audience is listening. Generally the best time to reach the unemployed is daytime and late night. Be sure your advertisement captures the attention of your viewers.

- **Cinema billboards.** Most people go to the movies from time to time, and for some people it is a second home. It may be expensive, but you will attract the attention of many potential candidates with a simple but eye-catching advertisement.

- **Direct mail.** By purchasing mailing lists through professional organizations, recruitment advertising agencies or mailing list companies, you can direct mail your recruitment message to many prospects.

- **Telemarketing.** This technique takes a little more thought because you will need people who are trained with your sales pitch to contact prospective candidates by telephone in much the same way that a recruiter works. This method can be very successful if it's done properly.

- **Job hotlines.** Many organizations are turning to voice mail and job hotlines to make it easier for candidates to find out about job openings. It's a great way to get the word out even when you're not available to speak to callers directly.

- **Layoffs/closings.** When businesses lay off or close operations, the market is generally flooded with candidates. Take advantage of the opportunity to interview those who meet your job requirements. You might even consider working in partnership with the businesses as these events occur to get first pick of qualified candidates.

- **Ex-offender programs.** There is always a need to find work once released from incarceration. Many employers have taken advantage of the opportunity to select the best candidates and work hand-in-hand with ex-offender programs in local communities. In some cases there's a financial incentive to do so.

- **Job lead organizations.** Increasingly, job seekers are turning to job lead organizations to help them learn how to sell themselves, as well as get tips on openings. They are a great resource for employers, many of whom are not aware of their existence.

- **On-campus interviews.** Soon-to-be college graduates are a source for candidates, and you can tap into this population by working with college placement offices to schedule time for interviews. You might even consider being part of a larger on-campus career fair.

- **Alumni associations.** Alumni often are active in assisting other graduates find employment. Most will be pleased that you thought to contact them and will work with you if you're interested.

- **Presentations to community organizations.** If your organization is asked to make a presentation of any kind, it's a good time to make it known that you are hiring. Word travels fast, and although no one in the audience may be interested, they will tell people who are looking for employment.

- **On-site interviews.** Interviews in malls and other public places is a great method of finding candidates you might not otherwise encounter. Some organizations actually have a permanent booth in shopping centers to attract potential future employees.

- **Airplane banner advertisement.** This method of recruitment may seem a little unusual to you, but some employers have found it to be effective, especially when advertising for entry-level positions in resort areas.

- **Door hangers.** This technique can be effective if you can quickly put your promotional piece on doors in apartment complexes, college dorms, or any place where you have large numbers of residents in one area.

- **Open houses.** What better way to promote your organization and the job opportunities within than to have an open house. You can advertise in the newspaper and conduct informal interviews on the spot. Those candidates in whom you have the most interest can be invited back later for a more in-depth interview.

- **Referral cards.** Some organizations have found success with referrals cards, which their managers carry and give to customer-oriented employees of businesses they patronize. For example, the card of a retail employer might say: "We are in need of customer-oriented sales associates. For more information call us." The card includes a contact name and phone number.

- **Scholarships.** As the competition heats up, businesses are offering low-interest loans, internships, work-study programs, and scholarships to entice students into a commitment of employment after graduation. The objective is to ensure that the organization meets its personnel needs by targeting potential employees at a younger age and nurturing their educational and professional development through college and even high school.

- **Branches of the U.S. military for those retiring or leaving.** The military is actively working to help its own find employment upon leaving the service. Don't overlook this resource of highly experienced personnel. All officers have advanced education, but that doesn't mean all enlisted personnel do not. From 75 to 80 percent of all military personnel are computer literate, and many are highly sophisticated in the field of electronics.

- **Former employees.** Unless former employees are not eligible for rehire, they should be considered for re-employment. They are a good source which is often overlooked. It also sends the message that this must be a great place to work if people want to come back.

- **Seniors (over 55) organizations.** The growing population of seniors continues to expand, many of whom are interested in full- or part-time employment. Take the initiative and contact senior organizations for qualified applicants.

- **Envelope stuffer advertisement.** Whether a message to your customers, vendors or current employees, envelope stuffers can be a very cost-effective and successful recruiting method. The flyer can be included in invoices and payroll checks, as well as with other information mailed out or distributed.

- **Celebrity hosted events.** If you want to attract attention and promote goodwill in your community at the same time, celebrities are a great way to do it while you recruit candidates. You probably wouldn't do this for a single entry-level position, but if you had 100 openings, it could be quite cost effective.

- **Job fairs.** Knowing your target market is the key to successful job fairs, which many employers have found especially valuable on college campuses and in areas of high unemployment.

- **Trade magazines and professional journals.** Both are a source for finding skilled professionals, but only if you plan ahead or have time to wait, as most are published monthly or quarterly.

- **Unsolicited resumes.** Every employer gets resumes even when there are not any openings. Don't discard resumes but file them by job category and refer to them first when you have a vacancy.

- **Professional associations.** Heavy duty networking takes place among members of professional associations. Notice of job opportunities are often published in newsletters. Announcements of positions available are frequently made at monthly or quarterly meetings. Most professional associations will be happy to work with you.

- **Transit advertising.** Advertising on buses and rapid transit systems or any other type of public transportation not only provides you with a place to advertise, but lets the rider know that your business can be reached without a car.

- **Magnetic signs.** You see them on the sides of cars and vans, so why not advertise job openings with your organization on a company vehicle? It's a great way to get the word out. Just be sure your brief advertisement sounds enticing.

- **Trade shows.** There is some good opportunity here, as you will interface with large numbers of people. Some trade shows are industry specific, while others like Chamber of Commerce trade shows target members, as well as outsiders, from a variety of backgrounds.

- **Posters with tear-off coupons.** This is a method of offering convenience to the job seeker, as all they have to do is tear off a coupon and mail it back. You can then schedule a telephone interview with those who are most qualified, or you can request a resume or completed application.

- **Bumper stickers.** Bumper stickers with a phone number and slogan will definitely attract attention and could be just what you need to get people to apply. Several that I have seen over the years are:

"Owner/Operators—We deliver the future!! "Call..."

"Stop! Look! Listen! We're hiring with full benefits. Call ..."

"I love my job. Give away free security systems and get paid! Call..."

"Attention Nurses: QUALITY CARE BEGINS WITH YOU. Call..."

"Jobs! Jobs! Jobs!—$10.00/hour. No experience necessary. Call..."

- **Job Databases.** Using information technology is one of the fastest ways to make it known that you have positions available. Job seekers are looking for opportunities and for many, Internet is where they start. For example, Web site Career Mosaic is run by Bernard Hodes Advertising Inc. in New York, which derives more than $200 million in annual income from upscale help-wanted ads, mostly in magazines and newspapers. Career Mosaic functions as an online classified-ads and job database. Internet users going to the site can view ads organized by type of work and corporate profiles of businesses that want to hire applicants. Ads stay active for 30 days and include the lavish graphics and hyperlinked text files typical of the Web. The site lists about 3,000 jobs daily in areas ranging from programming and engineering to accounting, marketing and sales.

There are so many ways to recruit creatively. I have only scratched the surface with these ideas. Don't get stuck in a rut if you are having trouble finding qualified people. Innovation could be the name of the game for your organization in finding the people you need.

T$P # 19: INVOLVE YOUR EMPLOYEES

Encourage your employees to get involved and make referrals. Although you always reserve the right to reject suggestions, getting your employees to help with recruiting has worked for many companies over the years. People associate with people like themselves. Your best employees will potentially make good referrals. If they are happy working in your organization, in many cases they will want to share those good feelings with their friends. In the last company at which I worked, I was always pleased to get referrals from employees, especially from those who were the best workers. They were proud to recommend their friends and family members to the company because it offered a good work environment and a competitive compensation and benefits package. For those same reasons, the company was in a position to be very selective about who was hired.

Two of the best reasons for getting your employees involved in recruiting are:

- First, you can get names of people who may be interested in working for you that you would not otherwise have encountered.

- Second, you've helped make your employees part of the process. Most people like to feel needed and appreciated, so why not take this opportunity to let them help you and feel good about what they're doing at the same time?

Employee referral programs are a great source for finding the right match to fill your job openings. Who better knows the organization and understands what the job involves than employees? Incentives can be commensurate with the level of the position or staffing difficulty. Consider paying a bonus to employees who refer people you ultimately hire. For example, if a company had 15 positions to fill and used an agency or a search firm to conduct a search, and paid them $10,000 per position filled, the company would spend a total of $150,000. Even if it paid only the cost of a block ad that runs every Sunday for 4 weeks at a cost of $1000 per ad, the cost would be $4,000. What better incentive to get your employees involved than saving money?

A reward system that pays employees an incentive can add excitement to the work place. This strategy gives your employees the opportunity to become creative in helping the company find good people for the job. However, the morale in the organization must be intact or the referral program will be unsuccessful. If your current employees are not happy, they won't have any enthusiasm for recruiting new people into the same bad environment. But if your organization's morale is good, a referral program that offers rewards is a win-win situation for everyone.

Some organizations offer the following rewards for recruitment, ranging from a token of appreciation to a significant gesture:

- Time off with pay.

- Eligibility for drawings.

- Cash.

- Savings bonds.

- Gift certificates.

- Trips.

- Prizes.

- Prime parking space.

Every program of this kind must have rules that are clearly defined so that all employees know what to expect. If the rules are unclear or perceived as unfair, employees will have no interest in participating.

I was involved in managing an incentive program that was already set up when I joined a company. It was effective in encouraging employees to submit names of potential candidates for open positions. The only fault I found with the plan was that many questions came up after the rules had been established. My predecessor was responsible for establishing the program and evidently did not consider the challenging questions that people would ask before the program kicked off. The problem was resolved by posting all of the rules and adding clarification to each. We had no more problems after that, but the warning shared is important to the success of any incentive program.

The main things to consider if you are planning a reward system for employees who recommend people for hire are:

- **Eligibility**–Decide who is eligible and who isn't. Typically human resource professionals would not be eligible, along with officers of the company and other managers with hiring authority.

- **Procedures**–The employee may be required to attach a card with his or her name to the application, the number of referrals may be limited and if the award is a vacation, the employee gets time off to take the trip in addition to regular vacation.

- **Parameters**–You will also want to establish rules in conjunction with the program that could include the system for distributing the cash award, the rights reserved by the organization to determine which referrals will be hired, and the confidentiality of decisions not to hire a candidate.

There are a number of ways in which an organization can gain from a referral program if it's managed well and promoted in a way that attracts attention and gets employees involved. From reducing the risk of a bad hiring decision and all of the headaches associated with it, to saving money, you have nothing to lose by trying this approach to recruiting as long as you have a good plan.

T$PS TO REMEMBER

1. Look for creative recruiting alternatives if you're having a problem finding good people. There are many proven methods that have worked well for employers; perhaps it's time to try something new.

2. Encourage employees to participate in filling vacancies by referring individuals who meet the job requirements.

3. Consider offering an incentive for successful "finds." Whether a simple gesture or substantial monetary award, decide on a way to make it worthwhile for employees to get involved.

4. Define eligibility, procedures and parameters before launching a referral program. You, as well as the employees, will gain from laying the groundwork up front.

CHAPTER 5

THE VALUE OF AGENCIES

As an employer, your job is to hire peak achievers, people who work smarter and harder. And since it costs about $100,000 to hire a $50,000 a year manager, you can't afford to make a mistake.
—Richard J. Pinsker
Executive Recruiter

Reputable employment agencies can save you time and money in finding candidates, especially those candidates who are difficult to locate. Whether using a search firm, executive recruiter, employment agency, temporary agency, or state employment service, keep in mind agencies vary in quality, approach and cost. If you decide to use an agency, you should be prepared to answer questions regarding what you're looking for as well as what you have to offer.

Some of the things you need to do in preparation for working with an agency include:

- Plan the scope of the search and whether or not you want the agency to conduct a local, regional, national, or international search.

- Decide how you want to handle relocation costs for the candidate.

- Be prepared for the information you will be asked to provide on benefits and salary, including bonus, commission, etc. You can expect that a good recruiter will want a complete picture of the job and the job requirements before beginning the search.

- Determine how much time you are willing to give the agency to conduct a thorough search.

- Check references on the agencies in which you are most interested.

- Sign only a contract with which you feel comfortable. Any questions you have should be resolved before you finalize the agreement.

A good agency can be invaluable in saving you time if you are working with a reliable and reputable service. A poor choice in an agency can bring lots of problems. For example, agencies are paid on commission and therefore, the quicker they fill the vacancy, the sooner they get paid. They are not always focused on finding the right match for you but rather on someone you are willing to accept. Be sure you define the parameters of your agreement before you get started.

As a human resource professional, I have worked with a variety of agencies from executive search firms to state employment services. They will find you if you are in a position of authority and could potentially gain from working with them and they with you. I've worked with some wonderful agencies including many temporary agencies who helped staff a new manufacturing facility in North Carolina when there was more work than we could handle. I've also worked with executive search firms on a retainer basis for hard-to-fill senior level positions. The local U.S. Department of Labor office also provided us with candidates on a regular basis.

T$P # 20: USE TEMPORARY AGENCIES

"Cost-effective," and "a good way to screen candidates," would be two of the best ways to describe some of the benefits of using temporary agencies. However, some employers fail to recognize that although temporary agencies can screen and hire for you, relying on them exclusively can be a mistake. By that I mean, for example, conducting a bad job interview or none at all because you assume the agency has done a thorough job in this area, especially if you have many positions that go from temporary to permanent. Shortchanging your involvement can lead to problems. I usually interview candidates even for temporary positions, just as I do for regular job openings, although the interviews are shorter and not as comprehensive.

Many businesses rely heavily on temporary agencies to fill positions in an effort to determine whether or not the candidate is the right fit for the job. The chance to try someone out on the job for a period of months is attractive. The fact that the employer pays no benefits and makes no commitments has kept temporary employment agencies busy.

Fortune magazine reports that the trend toward using temporary employees is exploding in popularity. Temporary agencies offer employers unskilled to highly skilled workers. The employer pays the agency, and the agency pays the employees. In the long run, money paid to temporary agencies can be far less expensive than hiring full time regular employees who are also eligible for benefits.

In preparing to work with a temporary agency to help you with staffing, develop a job description and prepare a detailed list of responsibilities. Decide how long you will need a temporary employee and budget to pay the agency. You might also want to find out if temporary personnel are required to sign a contractual agreement and how long they must work under the agreement before you could hire them permanently without penalty. Whether looking for an extra pair of hands or finding someone to fill in during an absence, planning ahead will ensure a smooth transition.

T$P # 21: CHECK OUT EMPLOYMENT AGENCIES

Different from temporary agencies, employment agencies who fill primarily full-time positions should also be considered if you don't have the time or staff to help you with recruiting or have hard-to-fill jobs. If you are willing to pay a fee for service, there are plenty of people who are willing to assist you.

Regardless of how you spend your recruiting dollars, whether with the help of an agency or on your own, it will cost you money to find qualified individuals. Employment agencies can provide you with clerical- and staff-level personnel. The employer and/or employee pays the fee, which is generally 20–25 percent of the candidate's starting salary. As an employer, you may never meet the agency representative in person since everything is usually handled by telephone. Expect quite a few referrals, but don't succumb to pressure from the agency to hire someone who does not meet your requirements.

T$P # 22: DON'T OVERLOOK EXECUTIVE RECRUITERS

Avoid questionable executive recruiters by checking them out in advance of an agreement. They can be an asset but only if you know what you're getting for your money. Most recruiters are reputable, but some are marginal in terms of the quality of service offered. I once used an executive recruiter who got pushy and demanding, trying to make it seem as though I really didn't know what I needed and that he did. He was verbally abusive to my secretary and when I found out and confronted him, he was livid. At that point I terminated our relationship.

Executive recruiters work on either a retainer or contingency basis to place entry-level to mid-level managers. They are expensive but can save you a great deal of time in screening and interviewing candidates. Executive recruiters charge up to 30 percent of the candidate's first year's salary, plus expenses.

T$P # 23: CONSIDER EXECUTIVE SEARCH FIRMS

Your answer to filling an especially difficult position could be in using an executive search firm. They (headhunters) work to fill senior level positions for client companies. Some specialize by industry or types of positions. Some firms are local while others have multiple locations and therefore access to a large computer database of applicants. They typically work on a retainer, so you will be billed one-half in advance, and even if the opening is filled through another source, you must pay the search firm according to your contract. Fees are 30–35 percent of the new hire's first year's salary plus bonuses and any expenses associated with the search. Using a search firm is not inexpensive but for certain hard-to-fill or executive-level positions, they are well worth the money spent.

T$P # 24: RECOGNIZE THE VALUE OF STATE EMPLOYMENT AGENCIES

State Employment Services provide referral services at no cost to employers or candidates. Candidates from entry to senior level are represented as are people who are both employed as well as unemployed. I know first hand that many employers don't recognize the value state agencies can provide in identifying candidates for skilled as well as unskilled positions. Don't miss out on the opportunity to get some help in recruiting at no cost to you.

T$PS TO REMEMBER

1. Agencies can be a valuable source of qualified candidates; just be sure you are happy with what you are getting before you sign a contract.

2. Be prepared to provide the agency with information concerning compensation, benefits, working conditions, hours and shift, etc.

3. Use temporary agencies to "try out" candidates whom you may want to hire for full time positions later.

4. Don't allow yourself to be pressured by a recruiter into hiring someone you don't want.

5. Consider using executive search firms to find candidates for senior-level and hard-to-fill positions.

6. Don't overlook the help offered by State Employment Services at no cost to you.

CHAPTER 6

PREPARE QUESTIONS IN ADVANCE

Mistakes in hiring for high-level management jobs can result in higher recruitment costs, unqualified managers, and wrongful termination suits. These are just a few of the consequences of poor hiring that make it essential to select managers carefully.
—Lisa McDaniel, SPHR
Human Resource Director,
Whidbey General Hospital, Coupeville, WA

We've all heard the expression: "People are our most important asset." Unfortunately, many people do not end up in the right jobs and are not an asset. They make everyone, including themselves, miserable. The selection process determines not only how well the candidate matches the job, it also impacts customer satisfaction, profitability and retention. Through carefully developed questions, you will want to identify what motivates candidates to do their best. You'll also need to discuss what the mutual expectations are and how you plan to work together to achieve those goals. Selecting and keeping a championship team is all about hiring the right people. You can get off to a good start by deciding what you need to know and what you want to ask of each candidate.

To avoid the problem of having a superficial discussion with a candidate rather than a meaningful interview, you need to develop or select questions that will elicit the information for making a good hiring decision. It also means avoiding questions related to race, color, religion, national origin, age, sex, and marital or family status, as well as disability. Be safe and develop questions around work experience, specific job skills, knowledge, and education.

It's important that you prepare interview questions well before the interview, and ideally it should be done after you've defined your specific job requirements. You can then develop questions that will get the answers you need to make a sound hiring decision, and you don't run the risk of leaving out anything important. Many hiring managers do a poor job of interviewing because they are unprepared and have no idea what they will ask in the interview.

Chapter 6 will help you prepare for job interviews by setting goals and developing questions that, in combination with good listening skills, will help you get the answers you need to determine whether or not you want to hire the candidate.

T$P # 25: SET GOALS FOR THE INTERVIEW

Prior to meeting the candidate face-to-face and beginning the interview, you must be prepared with a clear idea of what you are looking for. Without goals and a good idea of where you are going, it's like bowling in the dark. You can hear the sounds of the pins being hit or missed, but you have no way of knowing the score. By setting your goals up in advance, you have a much better chance of accomplishing what you set out to do. The more organized you are, the better impression you will make on the candidates.

I know a manager who, although she doesn't hire for her department more than twice each year, is well-prepared in planning what she needs to learn from each candidate. She doesn't have a human resource background, but she has always taken her hiring responsibilities seriously. She starts with a checklist that helps her focus on her specific goals.

Your checklist should reflect your goals and might include items such as:

*   Clarifying in your mind information on the resume or application regarding education and skills, and training or licenses required to perform the job.

- Finding out why candidates left previous employers. Was it for a better opportunity or were they asked to leave?

- Getting a feel for ability to get along with others even under highly stressful conditions. Is this person a team player?

- What leadership qualifications do the candidates possess? Can they supervise others?

- What will indicate to you that this individual can work under minimal supervision?

Questions like these come to mind when setting goals for the interview. They are not all-inclusive, but give you an idea of some of the things you may want to consider. The best way to assure that you meet your goals is to make them specific and clear, write them down and prioritize. It may mean you need to get back to basics in terms of how you organize yourself, but it's worth the effort when you've accomplished what you planned to do by the end of the interview.

T$P # 26: PREPARE OPEN QUESTIONS

Avoid closed questions and stick to those that will allow you to gather information about each candidate. A "yes" or "no" answer rarely yields anything useful unless, of course, you follow up with an open question. Start by developing a list of open questions which begin with "who?, what?, when?, where?, how?, or why?" Because they are probing, they will later help you decide whether or not candidates can do what they claim they can do. You can't afford not to get this kind of information. Open questions will help you recognize "cue" words in the answers which lend themselves to more open questions. The appendix contains sample interview questions. You will want, however, to soften questions that sound too direct. Richard A. Fear and Robert J. Chiron in their book, *The Evaluation Interview*, suggest that questions be "softened" by using introductory phrases and qualifying words such as:

- Is it possible that...?

- How did you happen to...?

- To what do you attribute...?

- Has there been any opportunity to...?

Each of these phrases takes away the sharp edge that questions tend to have, especially when asked in rapid succession. For example:

Too direct	Softened
I see on your application that you were fired from your last job; what did you do to cause that?	What events led up to you leaving your last job?
What kinds of problems do you have with your supervisor?	We all have times when we disagree with our supervisor. Can you tell me about a difference of opinion you had with your supervisor?
What do people criticize you for?	Criticism can be difficult to accept for most of us. How do you feel when someone criticizes you or your work?

Not only can we soften our questions through the words we choose, but we can also impact the way the questions sound by the tone of our voice and our body language. So much of what we say can be seen as offensive just by how we say it.

T$P # 27: DEVELOP BEHAVIOR-BASED QUESTIONS

Another type of question has to do with those which are designed to give the hiring manager a clear picture of how a candidate reacted in the past. Many managers find themselves short on information about the candidate because they don't ask behavior-based questions, most likely because they are not aware of the value the results will bring. Instead, they tend to ask hypothetical questions, which, in effect, invite the candidate to fabricate an answer. Some managers limit discussions to what's on the surface and never attempt to probe deeper for the reasons behind the candidates' decisions and actions.

Aside from being job-related and tied to the requirements of the position, behavior-based questions target past performance by asking the candidate to provide specific examples to support general statements. For example, if the candidate says "I'm good with customers," a good behavior-based question would be: "Can you give me an example of a time when you had to work with a difficult customer and succeeded?" With this question, you are asking the candidate to tell you about something he or she did in the past. Keep in mind, the more recent the example, the more reliable the predictor of future performance. Something that a candidate did in reference to a difficult customer when working as a 16-year-old newspaper carrier would not be as relevant as an example that took place when the candidate, after 25 years of management experience, handled a problem situation.

Behavior-based questions are an excellent way to find out how the candidate has done in a particular situation in the past. Take the time to develop a cross-section of questions that are both open and behavior-based before you start interviewing. Select behavior traits that you want to explore which are relevant to the position you want to fill and ask questions that will encourage candidates to discuss examples of those traits. Look for consistency, as that is where predictability will be the highest. You will find that you will feel much more comfortable and in control, and the candidate will also be more at ease. Appendix A of this book includes sample open, as well as behavior-based, questions.

T$PS TO REMEMBER

1. Set goals for the interview by working off of your checklist of issues you want to discuss or areas you want to explore.

2. Avoid closed questions, since the answers that follow will provide little useful information. Instead, focus on preparing open questions that will help you meet your goals for the interview.

3. Develop behavior-based questions to elicit information concerning how the candidate performed in the past. These questions will help you decide whether or not the candidate can do what is claimed.

4. Preparing your questions in advance will help you stay on track during the interview. Set the time aside before you meet the candidate to develop your job-related questions.

PART 2

SCREENING

According to the U.S. Department of Labor, if current trends continue, the United States will face an unprecedented shortage of skilled, educated workers by the year 2010 and will rank seventh in global productivity by 2015. With the end of the baby boom, qualified young workers will be increasingly scarce. Government projections indicate that by the year 2000, there will be 27 percent fewer 16- to 19-year-olds available for work than were available in 1980. Complicating matters further, new employees just out of school are different from the generations preceding them. Their work-related attitudes and expectations are different. Faced with these challenges, hiring managers must be ready, willing and able to put forth their best effort in screening out bad choices and those who think nothing of heading for greener pastures soon after joining the organization.

How you screen for the "cream of the crop" will depend to a great degree on your skills. The screening process is meant to be quick as you review information on resumes, applications and cover letters. After you've looked at several hundred resumes, they all begin to look alike. Job seekers read the same job hunting books, listen to audio tapes and watch videos designed to give the unemployed the inside secrets to preparing resumes that get action. They are coached by the experts in resume writing techniques; it's no wonder that the job of screening for the hiring manager may seem like a nightmare. Completed applications will provide you with additional insights, depending upon what kind of information your form requests. Whether you are using an off-the-shelf form or have developed your own, federal and state labor laws govern what you may and may not ask.

Cover letters will also provide another perspective on the applicant. For example, one of the first things I notice when screening cover letters is grammar, spelling and punctuation. If I spot typos and run-on sentences, I'm immediately concerned because I think of the cover letter and resume as the candidate's best foot forward. Mistakes speak volumes. When I see that a cover letter has been photo-copied and undoubtedly mass-mailed, I know the candidate takes short cuts in areas of importance and that concerns me.

The last part of screening is critical as it will save you an enormous amount of time and money with a 20- or 30-minute telephone call, a step I never fail to take. The telephone interview will help you make a decision as to whether or not you want to invest more time in a candidate with a personal interview. I've seen hiring managers ignore or forget this step too often. I'm reminded of a manager who decided to by-pass the human resources department and hire a supervisor on his own. His recruitment advertisement was broad and brought several hundred resumes from around the country. He found two candidates he liked based on their resumes, each of whom lived 1,000 miles away. Without a telephone interview, he invited each of them to fly to Raleigh, NC, on a company-paid airline ticket. After 20 minutes with each candidate, he immediately knew that neither one was suited for the job he had in mind. The expensive mistake depleted his recruiting budget for the position, and two candidates left confused and angry.

As you prepare to screen, you will want to sort resumes and/or applications into three stacks:

- Meets all requirements.

- Meets most requirements.

- Does not meet enough requirements to justify a face-to-face interview.

As you sort resumes, you may occasionally come across resumes of candidates who look too good to be true. They appear to have impeccable credentials; they meet most but not all of the job requirements you've identified. You may have a nagging feeling that something is not right. Place them in a stack labeled "meets most requirements." Don't exclude them, but proceed cautiously in the interview. By that I mean, when conducting the interview later, do an especially thorough job of interviewing the individual to verify that what was stated in the resume is true.

CHAPTER 7

EVALUATE WHAT YOU SEE AND HEAR

The most important thing you should know about resumes is that they are like mirrors in a funhouse: They offer a distorted image of reality whose main function is to deceive the eye.

—Martin Yate
Consultant and Author

Many organizations have come to terms with the fact that there is a definite relationship between bad hiring decisions and turnover and that the hiring manager is in the best position to control this loss. Businesses often fight the battle of discipline and eventual termination. They struggle with personnel issues and want to know how to avoid problems in the future. There is no doubt that making the right hiring decision from the beginning can greatly influence what employees do from the first day on the job forward. Although bad hiring decisions may never be completely eliminated, there is no need to blindly accept a bad fit. As you read further on how to prepare yourself for screening resumes, cover letters and applications, you will learn how to become more effective in reviewing all three. First, you will screen these documents against your job requirements. Later, you will review them again immediately prior to the interview so that you can discuss specifics with the candidate.

The main reasons for conducting a more complete evaluation before meeting the candidate are:

- It will help you stay organized and follow your agenda if you have a plan regarding what you want clarified on the documents.

- The more you know ahead of time, the better prepared you are to develop or select questions appropriate for each candidate.

- Being prepared for questioning will help some of the stress or nervousness associated with interviewing.

Some documents will strike you as funny or off-the-wall. Others will be unnecessarily long, while many will be so brief or incomplete that they tell you almost nothing about the candidate. Probably the most memorable of cover letters I have seen was from a candidate who made his living as a writer and advertising agent. It was most unusual and clever. Although he was not qualified for the job, I did call him to find out more about his advertising background as the company I worked for was also looking for a creative director.

After completing your first screening of resumes, cover letters and applications, you will contact the best candidates by telephone and conduct a phone interview. A step that is frequently skipped, telephone interviews will save you time and money. Following the telephone interview, you will know whom you want to invest in further with a face-to-face interview.

T$P # 28: LEARN HOW TO SCREEN APPLICATIONS

Hiring managers who are anxious to quickly screen a pile of documents and move on, often make mistakes. Sometimes the selection process is no better than leaving choices to chance or choosing at random. As many as 50 percent of your candidates can be eliminated when you screen applications. This process allows you to later focus your efforts on interviewing only those individuals who meet your job requirements. Some organizations mail applications to candidates upon request, while other businesses require candidates to complete applications at the employment site so that there is no doubt concerning who completed the form. As a result, errors, sloppiness and inconsistencies can be attributed to the candidate and taken into consideration when evaluating. The decision is yours; for unskilled and semi-skilled positions, I like to have candidates complete an application at the company and leave it with the receptionist.

Applications are typically printed or handwritten just prior to the first meeting with the employer. The interviewer can immediately spot missing information and observe neatness. The information on an application is straightforward and devoid of any of the embellishment that a resume provides, and it requests accuracy and truthfulness. Most applications contain a statement such as "I understand that false or misleading information may result in termination of employment."

T$P # 29: PRACTICE SCREENING RESUMES

Screening resumes and screening applications is very similar. If I told you I could effectively screen 350 resumes in two hours, would you believe me? It can be done, and every hiring manager should use a method that will allow quick and reliable screening of resumes. I accomplish this feat by screening with a highlighter and looking for everything that matches my requirements. I review career objective, work experience and educational history. Only those who meet the requirements pass the test.

A resume is the job seeker's "calling card." Many are carefully prepared; some candidates create their own while others use a resume writing service. Each is hoping to survive the "cut" and be one of a handful selected for an interview. It's no secret that resumes should be typed and free of spelling and grammatical errors. The candidate decides what will be included on the resume and most likely includes his or her best credentials. Information on a resume often includes career objective, work experience and educational background. Some of what I call "old fashioned" resumes still include personal information such as marital status, date of birth, height, weight, etc. If personal information appears, be careful not to screen out someone based on that information as it could be seen as discriminatory.

In screening resumes you will want to look for clues to the candidate by considering the following:

- Is there a career objective, if so, is it specific or general? Candidates who know what they want and are focused in their job search efforts will have a very clear career objective. That immediately tells me the individuals are not applying for any job that comes along, but are selective and know what they want.

• Does the resume include accomplishment statements or is it just a job description? Does it indicate that the candidate is budget conscious, profit-minded and successful in reducing costs? The more achievements in a resume, the more I want to read further.

• Does the format of the resume do a good job of getting the author's message across? Is the resume in chronological or functional form or a combination of the two? If it's a functional resume, do you get the impression that the candidate is hiding something? Functional formats provide a good cover for gaps in work history and lack of specific experience.

• Is the resume more than two pages and are the words crowded together or is there enough white space to make it easy to read? Winston Churchill once delivered a one-hour speech. He was asked how long it took to write, to which he replied "two hours." When the person he was speaking to was surprised, Churchill said: "I could have written a half-hour speech if I'd had four hours to write it." You might assume that if a candidate has a long resume, that he may also be long-winded in the board room. You'll know more when you conduct a telephone screen.

• Evidence of writing ability can often be seen in well-written resumes with action verbs starting each accomplishment statement. Is it written in the proper tense, with no dangling participles, or is it an English teacher's nightmare?

These are some of the items that I look for when screening resumes. The overall appearance provides a first impression. TIP # 30 includes some additional things you will want to consider.

T$P # 30: RECOGNIZE "RED FLAG" WARNINGS

Taking everything on the resume and/or application at face value without an in-depth interview is dangerous because candidates police their own documents. Anyone who decides to falsify what they offer as evidence of work experience, skills and education can easily do so on a resume or application. Dishonest documents can be a real problem, especially if you don't recognize them as being phony. Some research suggests that almost one-half of all candidates lie, distort or in some way fabricate information on resumes and applications. In reality, many resumes are vague, not to mention the phenomenon of academic credential fraud. Recent research found that more than one-half million people in the United States have bogus degrees. In addition, one-third of U.S. employers routinely hire individuals without requesting any academic documents for verification. No wonder organizations are making bad hiring decisions.

There are many bits of information on resumes and applications which should immediately get your attention and warn you of potential problems. Be aware that some candidates re-invent their employment histories on resumes. In other words, don't take everything you read at face value. A better way to get the information you need is to ask every candidate to complete a standard application. And don't forget, there is a lot you won't know about a candidate just by looking at a resume. The face-to-face interview will answer a lot of questions generated by the resume or application.

However, just because you see something questionable, doesn't mean that you will necessarily screen that individual out. Warnings are there so that you can follow up with the candidate and ask questions until you are satisfied with what you hear.

"Red Flag" warnings include the following:

- Be concerned when information is omitted. It is more difficult to spot on resumes because the candidate is in control of what the resume includes. On an application, omissions are easier to see and should also be addressed.

- Don't overlook qualifiers such as "had exposure to," "have knowledge of," and "assisted with." You will want to ask further questions to determine if the candidate actually did the work or was merely a spectator.

- Candidates who indicate that they "attended" a school may be hoping that you don't recognize that they did not graduate. Ask what is meant by "attended."

- Dates which are inconsistent should be immediately suspect.

- Reason for leaving a former employer is sometimes included on applications. When a candidate writes "personal," you have the right as a prospective employer to find out what is meant by "personal."

- Vague answers, such as listing the state the employer was in and not the full address are reason for concern.

- Inconsistencies in salary history should be challenged.

- Regressive work history (or appearing to step backwards in a career or job duties) should also be questioned, especially if the candidate is willing to accept a job which pays considerably less than the previous job.

- Changing jobs frequently should also be carefully probed. You will want to get a good feel for the candidate's stability, reliability, expectations, and maturity. There may be a very good reason for the changes, but you won't know for sure unless you ask.

- When all references listed are out of business, be suspicious.

T$P # 31: LEARN HOW TO REVIEW COVER LETTERS

Most resumes will be accompanied by a cover letter and can be as revealing as the resume itself. Yet many hiring managers don't read the cover letter or don't know how to evaluate what they read. Learn how to read between the lines and get some additional clues about the candidate.

Whether "Gentlemen," "To Whom It May Concern," "Dear Sir/ Madam," or something in between, the salutation immediately tells you about the candidate's level of sophistication. Savvy candidates will make it a point to find out to whom the letter and resume is being sent and personalize it by addressing the receiver by name, i.e., "Dear Ms. Banks." However, names of employees are often not given out readily over the phone by organizations. Blind ads provide nothing other than a post office box. As a result, you will see a variety of salutations.

Beyond the salutation, a good cover letter will mention the organization's specific requirements and the candidate's strengths as they relate to those needs. If you have asked for salary requirements in your advertisement, that information may also be included, although many candidates will ignore your request for salary data because they know that employers use that information to screen candidates out.

T$P # 32: PRE-SCREEN BY TELEPHONE

Pre-screening candidates by telephone prior to the face-to-face interview is an invaluable step that should never be overlooked. A tremendous amount of information can be obtained with a few questions and by listening carefully to how the answer is articulated. Age and race as well as physical appearance are inconsequential when you can't see the candidate. It allows you to be more objective and requires you to listen carefully to what is said.

Save time and money by telephone screening all candidates who meet your qualifications as stated in resumes and applications. Call the candidate and ask if it is convenient to talk. It's possible that the candidate is not able to speak with you at that time. If that's the case, offer to call back at a time that would be more convenient. Use a list of prepared interview questions and stick to them. This is a good time to ask specific questions regarding work experience and level of skill.

Before you know what you want and need, you might want to use an evaluation form with all candidates as it will help you to organize your thoughts and compare candidates. You'll also want to know what you are going to say to establish rapport at the beginning of the interview as well as what you plan to say about the organization and the job. Setting aside uninterrupted time to interview by telephone is also important.

Allow 20–30 minutes for this pre-screen interview. There may be exceptions for candidates who express that they are no longer interested in being considered. The other exception would be if you felt a need to talk further in order to get the information to make a decision regarding a face-to-face interview. At times the pre-screen may be an hour or more because the candidate lives out of town and the interviewer wants to make sure that an investment in travel expenses and time will be well spent.

Telephone screening is difficult but important. It's difficult because you cannot see the candidates or their non-verbal reactions. It is important because it will save you time and money.

The following tips will help you conduct an effective telephone interview:

- Draft a list of open questions. These questions should be based upon the skills and experience you need. Unless the candidate meets your expectations by telephone, there is no need to go any further.

- Review the resume and/or application and highlight anything you want to discuss.

- Know what you are looking for and review job requirements immediately prior to the telephone interview. Once you've placed the call, you should be prepared to begin the interview.

- Introduce yourself and ask if it is convenient to talk. Give the candidate the option of returning your call later.

- Get to the point immediately and share your agenda, including the approximate amount of time you plan to spend with the candidate by phone. I might say something like:

    "My name is Carol Hacker. I'm the credit manager at XYZ company. I'm calling about your interest in our opening for a credit analyst. Is this a convenient time to talk?"

If the candidate says "yes," I would say: "I'd like to spend about thirty minutes talking about your work experience as related to the job we have available. How does that sound?" If the candidate says "no," I would ask when my call could be returned or when I could call back.

- Build rapport by being upbeat and friendly. Smile and stand while talking if you want to project maximum energy.

- Listen carefully. Some candidates may act pretty turned-off or rude until they understand who you are and why you are calling. Telephone manners immediately become apparent in the phone interview.

- Conclude the interview by telling the candidate what will happen next.

After you've screened resumes, cover letters and applications, you are ready for a very important step—the telephone screen. Often neglected, this interview will allow you to get to know the candidate better and when you are through, you will know the following:

- How serious the candidate's interest is in the job.

- How well the candidate communicates verbally.

- How persuasive the candidate is in selling himself or herself to you.

- Whether or not there is any "chemistry" between the two of you.

- Whether or not you want to invest in a face-to-face interview.

With the telephone interview, there is little room for personal bias based on how the candidate looks. You cannot see the individual over the phone, and you won't be able to make a snap judgement based on physical appearance.

T$PS TO REMEMBER

1. Screening resumes, applications and cover letters is an important step in the process but reaps its own rewards as you begin to construct a profile of the candidate.

2. Screen with a highlighter and sort into three stacks—meets all requirements, meets most requirements, does not meet requirements.

3. Recognize signs that indicate candidates may not be what they appear to be. Later, explore those issues that are troublesome during the interview until you are satisfied you have enough information to make a decision.

4. Watch for sloppiness, spelling errors and poor grammar in forming an impression of the candidate.

5. Use the telephone to pre-screen candidates who meet your requirements on paper. In 20 to 30 minutes you should know if a face-to-face interview should be scheduled.

6. Decide what you're going to say to get the telephone interview started, always giving the candidate the option of calling you back at a more convenient time.

7. In the telephone interview, work from a list of prepared questions that are based upon the skills and work experience required.

CHAPTER 8

PRE-EMPLOYMENT TESTING

Numerous studies have shown that hiring better people will result in more productive employees who are likely to stay longer and be less prone to causing accidents or committing acts of violence
—*The Pryor Report*

Pre-employment testing many be controversial, but it is definitely here to stay. Tests are not illegal as long as you use professionally developed tests which do not discriminate. Written instructions must be provided, and the test must always be given under the same conditions. Reliability and validity is important to ensure that the tests help select the candidates who can be successful on the job. The EEOC requires that tests conform to the Uniform Guidelines for Employee Selection Procedures to ensure that no adverse impact exists. Even with all of the guidelines in place, testing is not a magic solution for hiring the people you need to do the job.

There are several highly publicized court cases surrounding the use of pre-employment testing. In ruling against the defendant, the Court established two major points in Griggs v. Duke Power. First, it's not sufficient to show a lack of discriminatory intent if the selection instrument discriminates against one group more than another. Second, the burden of proof falls upon the employer to show that any employment requirement is directly job-related. In Albemarle Paper v. Moody, the Court reaffirmed the idea that any "test," including performance appraisals used for selecting or promoting employees, must be a valid predictor for a particular job.

In Hester v. Southern Railway Company, a black female was denied a clerical job based on non-validated aptitude tests and a highly subjective interview. The District Court commented on the faulty nature of the interview, based on its lack of "formal guidelines, standards, or instructions." The decision, however, was overturned by the Court of Appeals based on the lack of clear proof of a prima facie case of discrimination.

In Washington v. Davis, the Court ruled that the Civil Service exam could be used to select police officers, even though it excluded a disproportionately greater percentage of black applicants, because a statistical validation had shown that test scores were significantly related to training scores. The many state and federal laws that govern pre-employment testing, along with privacy rights laws and negligence laws, protect the individual's rights to equal opportunity without regard to race, color, sex, religion, national origin, and physical handicap.

To avoid liability, employers must be able to show that:

- Test questions do not screen out a disproportionately large number of minorities.

- All tests are directly related to the specific position you are trying to fill. You may be asked to prove that there is a direct correlation between what you require of candidates and what is actually needed for success in the job.

- The level of difficulty of pre-employment tests cannot be unreasonable. Unnecessarily high standards often exclude qualified minorities who don't have formal education but who can still perform the job.

Many organizations are preventing mis-hires as a result of paper and pencil tests. If you plan to spend your organization's money on pre-employment testing for job applicants, you need to be prepared to evaluate vendor claims of "valid," "reliable," and "cost effective." Many tests have been developed by psychologists, people who are experts in the field, so how can the average hiring manager be expected to interpret the results of devices such as these?

You will want to check the credentials and reputation of the vendor. If the test developer is called to court, the first questions asked will be about the vendor's qualifications. Asking for a resume from the test's author and verification of education is advisable. In many cases, you will be talking about an author who holds a Ph.D., which in most states, is the minimum requirement for being considered a psychologist. Next, you should research the author's publication record. Find out what has been printed in professional journals. Checking the test's reputation is very important and similar to checking a candidate's references. You will also want to examine the test's underlying research.

As you can see, knowing that a test is appropriate and valid and that the credentials of the author are impeccable is a time-consuming task. Don't take a chance that the tests your organization are using to screen applicants could land you in court. Without a background in psychological testing, it is not hard to be convinced of the worth of a pre-employment test. There are lots of good sales people depending upon you for a living.

T$P #: 33 EVALUATE THE NEED FOR TESTING

Employers who believe that everyone must be tested perhaps should re-think their decision and take the time to evaluate the actual need for testing. Often there really isn't a need, but testing is seen as an absolute answer to uncertainty. When hiring managers don't feel comfortable interviewing and making hiring decisions, it's easy to believe that giving applicants a test will ease the burden of having to make a decision. What some advocates of testing forget is that tests have limitations. No test could possibly measure everything that is needed to successfully handle the job. Even those tests that are considered to be the most reliable have margins of error. Pre-employment tests were never meant to be an easy answer to hiring dilemmas, but are intended to supplement the selection process.

As you evaluate the need for testing, you will want to consider several factors:

• Is this the only way you can get the information you need regarding the candidate's skills?

- Will the test be a valid predictor of job success?

- Could some other selection method work just as well or better?

- Is the financial cost justified in relationship to the information you will get?

- Could a skilled interviewer get the same information from interviewing the candidate?

If you decide there is a need for testing, then you will want to know how to select pre-employment tests as well as what risks are involved. Pre-employment testing can expose employers to negligent hiring claims by candidates who are rejected. Privacy issues are also a potential liability, e.g., medical examinations or information. Some instruments are looked upon as an invasion of privacy when they cover personality and honesty.

T$P # 34: LEARN HOW TO SELECT PRE-EMPLOYMENT TESTS

In 1978, the EEOC, the Office of Personnel Management, the Department of Justice, and the Department of Labor adopted and published a document entitled *Uniform Guidelines on Employee Selection Procedures,* more commonly referred to as Uniform Guidelines. The Uniform Guidelines are designed to provide the framework for determining the proper uses of tests and other selection procedures used for any employment decision.

Seen as the cornerstone of the screening process, some managers argue that testing is the only way to screen out undesirables. The fact is that pre-employment tests can be dangerous in the hands of unqualified people who don't know how to select tests and/or use them properly or who use testing as the sole reason for rejecting candidates. Tests that measure the candidate's knowledge and skill in a specific area such as accounting, office administration, data processing, etc. are the best indicators of ability to perform the job. You should, however, seek legal counsel before implementing any type of pre- or post-employment testing. The process of validation is complicated and should be conducted by an expert.

Some of the questions you need to answer before you test are:

- Will you test every candidate?

- Was the test developed on the basis of a job analysis?

- Was testing done on incumbents to test the test?

- Does the test measure job performance?

- Does the test measure major job responsibilities of the job?

- Does the test have an adverse impact on a protected group?

- Is the test site consistent in terms of space, noise, light conditions, temperature, time given to complete the test, administrator giving the test, and scoring procedures?

- What percentage of people pass the test?

- What percentage of those who pass are minorities?

Many organizations successfully use professionally developed pre-employment screening devices, some of which fall into the following categories:

- **Honesty**–Designed to measure either general traits of the candidate's honesty or specific traits such as trustworthiness, tendency toward stealing and integrity, they are used more frequently as a result of the passing of the Polygraph Protection Act, which makes polygraph tests illegal. These tests are relatively inexpensive and easy to administer but not without risk, with the burden of proof always on the employer. The National Business Crime Information Network reports that American businesses lost more than $200 billion dollars in 1994 to cash and merchandise thefts committed by employees.

- **Achievement**–Designed to test the candidate's knowledge and skill in a specific area, achievement tests are also regulated by state and federal statutes. Be sure it measures what it should and does not have an adverse impact on protected classes of applicants.

- **Personality**—Seen as an invasion of privacy instrument, personality tests can cost anywhere between $75 and $300. A 1989 California Superior Court case (Soroka v. Target Stores) was filed involving a class-action suit against an employer by people who refused to take a pre-employment personality test and were thus not considered for employment. They alleged that the test violated their state Constitutional rights to privacy through discrimination and negligent misrepresentation on the basis of the test asking questions about religious and sexual beliefs. Personality tests should be used only in special cases, but not without being absolutely sure about their reliability and validity.

- **Psychological**—Provides a psychological profile of the candidate that can be seen as discriminatory. Many states have laws that protect job seekers from tests of this type. If you have any doubts as to whether or not the test you have in mind is appropriate, seek legal counsel.

- **Polygraph**—Designed to determine truthfulness, the federal Polygraph Protection Act of 1988 was enacted to protect an individual's rights regarding free speech, privacy, self-incrimination, and the right to be free from illegal search and seizure. It is against the law to use this test defined as: "any mechanical or electrical process used to render a diagnostic opinion regarding honesty."

- **Handwriting analysis**—Designed to learn more about the candidate's traits, talents, abilities, strengths, weaknesses, emotions, and intellect through handwriting, they can be seen as discriminatory and in violation of an individual's right to privacy. Critics believe that there is no scientific basis for conclusions drawn from the results.

- **Medical examinations**—Designed to test the candidate's physical abilities and limitations, state and federal laws governing medical exams make it illegal to discriminate against a candidate based on a physical or mental impairment as long as the candidate is otherwise qualified to perform the essential functions of the job.

- **Drug and alcohol tests**–More than half of all companies in the United States conduct drug and alcohol screening tests before hiring. Neither encouraged nor forbidden by the Americans With Disabilities Act (ADA), drug and alcohol testing can help an employer avoid hiring candidates who pose a health and/or safety risk to themselves and others. Former drug users or alcoholics who have been rehabilitated or who are participating in a supervised rehabilitation program are protected under the ADA and must be given consideration for the job.

In larger organizations that have a human resource manager, that individual is responsible for seeing to it that any of the above-mentioned tests are not only valid but administered in a way that is not discriminatory. In smaller organizations, the person responsible for testing needs to be completely knowledgeable in this area. If you are not comfortable with the tests you are using, you should seek legal assistance immediately. A charge based on discrimination because of preferential treatment during the pre-employment testing process or use of an invalid instrument could cost your organization thousands to defend.

Should you decide to pre-test, never use the results as the sole basis for your decision to hire or not to hire. Be aware of the many testing companies who are ready to sell you pre-packaged selection tests. If you do decide to test, use the information as only one step in evaluating the candidate. The face-to-face interview is still the most effective way to determine whether or not the candidate is the right choice for you and your organization.

T$P # 35: USE PRE-EMPLOYMENT TESTS WITH CAUTION

The pre-employment test is only one of three ways to evaluate candidates. Interviewing and checking references are the other two. Managers who see testing as the most reliable selection method are fooling themselves. There are too many variables that can make a test invalid. The typical manager may not recognize these pitfalls and that can be dangerous. I am not against pre-employment testing, but I am concerned when tests get into the hands of inexperienced people or an invalid instrument is used to determine whether or not someone passes or fails.

I often see organizations who don't recognize the limitations and hazards of pre-employment tests, such as a company with whom I consulted a number of years ago. They found themselves facing a lawsuit that claimed discrimination and invasion of privacy. Although state laws vary with regard to individual protection, this company was in blatant violation. They developed their own "honesty" and "personality" tests believing because their human resource manager was a licensed psychologist, that they were within their rights to administer the tests and that they were protected because of the educational credentials of the human resource manager. Their presumptions cost them $500,000 in damages and legal fees.

Other examples of organizations that did not comply with discrimination laws resulted in the following highly publicized lawsuits: Watson v. Fort Worth Bank & Trust (1988) and EEOC v. Atlas Paper Box Company (1989). Each of these cases dealt with discrimination and the selection testing process.

Problems with testing vary and include the following:

- **Some candidates play "beat the system."**

   There are some very clever job seekers who want to trick you into believing that they are the perfect choice because they did "well" on the test. They may be experts at taking tests and answering questions to their best advantage. Many tests have built in safeguards against individuals who try to manipulate the test, but others do not. How will you know the manipulator from the honest test taker? The average manager may not recognize a manipulator. The type of test you use holds the best chance for identifying those who try to cheat the test.

- **Some people are lousy test takers.**

   Some people do not take tests well. They become nervous and fail miserably when faced with a pencil, paper and a lot of questions. They may end up eliminated from the next step in the hiring process, perhaps unnecessarily. Is it fair to exclude candidates because they freeze up when taking a test?

- **Some tests are discriminatory.**

  Would you know a biased instrument from a test that was
  appropriate and valid? If you cannot answer a confident "yes"
  to this question, you have no business administering pre-employment tests.

- **Some tests are extremely complicated to administer and
  interpret.**

  Tests that require assistance from an outside source such as a
  psychologist can be very costly. Do you have the money to pay
  for expertise? If you don't and are not willing to pay the costs,
  maybe you need to reconsider.

- **Some tests do not accurately predict success on the job.**

  If the test does not measure skills, abilities and knowledge, you
  have a problem. The Equal Employment Opportunity Commission (EEOC) and the courts require that pre-employment
  tests must be valid for the particular job being tested.

T$P # 36: UNDERSTAND THE IMPLICATIONS OF "ADVERSE IMPACT"

If you decide to test, you will need to comply with federal and state
laws and regulations. Pre-employment tests do not have to be validated
if they do not show adverse impact on any race, sex or ethnic group.
However, if the test you plan to use does have an adverse impact on a
protected group, the test must be validated by proving its relevance to job
requirements and performance. The "four-fifths rule" gauges adverse
impact. Adverse impact is shown if the selection rate for any race, sex or
ethnic group is less than four-fifths or 80 percent of the rate for the group
with the highest selection rate.

For Example:

Hypothetically, of the 150 people who apply for a job, 90 are
white and 60 are hispanic. Of those hired, 63 are white and 18
are hispanic. The selection rate for hispanics equals 30 percent

(18 divided by 60), and the selection rate for whites is 70 percent (63 divided by 90). The white group had the highest selection rate. Consequently, the cut off for determining adverse impact is 56 percent (70 percent times 80 percent). Since the hispanic selection rate is less than 56 percent, adverse impact exists.

For Example:

If 35 percent of all qualified black applicants, compared to 50 percent of white applicants, pass a written selection test, the selection rate for blacks is 70 percent of the rate for whites, and the test has an adverse impact. If a selection procedure or hiring qualification is shown to have an adverse impact, then the employer must prove either the business necessity or the job-relatedness of the screening criteria used. In addition, your selection procedures must be documented and broken down into race, ethnic and sex categories. If adverse impact is found, you must conduct a validity test. If you cannot prove that the test is valid, you must modify your selection procedures to eliminate adverse impact.

T$P # 37: CONSIDER USING WORK SAMPLES

Many hiring managers don't know what a "work sample" is and therefore, have never used it in screening candidates. Work samples are tests of skill and allow you to find out if the candidate has the skill to do the things you need done. Used properly, they are a good barometer for measuring specific skills. Work samples can assess many abilities including setting priorities, making decisions, handling conflict, and communicating, as well as more specific technical abilities. Exercises are often simulations based upon specific skills needed to do the job. Training in observation and evaluation techniques are crucial to the success of using work samples.

There are several ways to go about gathering work samples:

• The first is to ask the individual to bring a sample of his or her work to the interview.

- The second is to ask the candidate to perform work that is typical of the kind of work he or she would be doing on the job. Under controlled conditions, when each candidate is asked to complete the same exercise, the results can be very revealing.

For example, candidates for an administrative position could be asked to prepare a report using the computer, or an individual applying for a position as a graphic artist could be asked to sketch an idea for a hypothetical new product line. The point here is to give the candidate the chance to show you what he or she can do in the time allowed. Comparing results among candidates is another effective tool in the hiring process. The caution here is be sure what you are asking someone to do is directly related to what is actually going to be done on the job. All work samples must also be valid with no "adverse impact."

T$PS TO REMEMBER

1. Any tests that screen out minorities as compared to other groups are illegal under EEO guidelines.

2. Seek the help of an expert if you are unsure about how to administer tests.

3. To avoid liability, you must be able to show that skill tests are valid and a good predictor of future work performance.

4. Recognize that there are a number of inherent problems with using pre-employment tests.

5. Drug and alcohol tests are used by more than 50 percent of employers to screen out potential problem employees. The ADA does not protect employees or applicants who are currently engaged in illegal use of drugs. An alcoholic is considered a safety threat and is not protected either.

6. Apply the "four-fifths rule" in gauging adverse impact with regard to race, sex and ethnic group.

7. Use work samples to test candidates but only if the test is valid and does not discriminate against a protected group of people.

PART 3

THE INTERVIEW

Most job seekers are more prepared for employment interviews than the people who hire them. It's no wonder that a quick trip to your local bookstore will show you that the shelves are filled with books about every phase of the hiring process. Outplacement firms coach candidates on what to expect and how to respond to even the toughest probes. Image consultants counsel job seekers on the "do's" and "don'ts" of interview etiquette and how to dress to impress. A highly prepared candidate comes face-to-face with an inexperienced interviewer and that often means trouble.

Unprepared managers generally conduct ineffective interviews, and ineffective interviews ultimately lead to bad hiring decisions. Some interviewers don't know what to ask and risk leaving the quality of the interview process to chance. This laissez-faire attitude usually leads to disastrous and costly results. It is your responsibility as a hiring manager to develop the comprehensive skills needed to conduct an effective interview. These skills are as important as any other job responsibility you have. You will need to do a lot of groundwork before interviewing both well-prepared candidates and those who are qualified professionally but lack good interview skills.

As you prepare, remember the importance of basic interview etiquette. You not only represent your organization, but your reputation is also at stake. It is your duty to maintain a positive image. When the interview is over, the impression the candidate leaves with will ultimately impact his or her decision to accept or reject your offer. The best public relations that organizations have going for themselves are honest, effective and well-trained hiring managers, who are conscious of maintaining a quality reputation for their organizations, as well as for themselves, when interfacing with candidates.

Bad hiring decisions inevitably become a human resource replacement issue and include both direct and indirect costs. Following enactment of the Civil Rights Act of 1991, successful claimants may demand jury trials and recover compensatory damages and punitive damages up to $300,000, plus money for expert witnesses who testify at the trial. It is your responsibility as the hiring manager to make defensible hiring decisions. You can't do that unless you know how to interview effectively. In addition, the success of your recruiting efforts and your overall commitment to training once the candidate joins your organization will soon be evident in your turnover rate.

Getting a feel for how the candidate thinks and solves problems requires more than an informal conversation or wishful thinking. The in-depth interview should probe the candidate's accomplishments as well as weaknesses. Questions and your own observations regarding the candidate's interpersonal skills, level of maturity, personality traits, interest in your organization, and willingness to accept responsibility are an acceptable method for finding out about the candidate. Forget the excuses about not having time to do it right the first time. Make a commitment to yourself and your organization that you will never again walk into an interview unprepared.

It's time again to take a serious look at the tremendous cost potential of a bad hiring decision which includes but is not limited to lost opportunities, poor publicity, increased turnover, wrongful discharge litigation, wasted time, decline in morale, etc. Bad interviewing techniques and sloppy habits may also force you to hire someone you had no intention of employing.

A $25 million dollar company in the Southwest estimated their costs in bad hiring decisions during the past three years to be in excess of 1 million dollars! Their business was a revolving door of people as they scurried to hire as quickly as they fired. Employees who were not fired quit in disgust. At one point halfway through the fiscal year, their rate of turnover was 83 percent. No business can survive for long with a track record like that. They finally made some drastic changes in their hiring practices and set a goal of *zero* turnover. They had no choice. That decision ultimately saved the business.

A nonprofit organization said their costs of bad hiring decisions ran over $500,000 during a two-year period. Their board of directors was furious and forced them to change their approach to hiring and decision-making. It wasn't enough because they had no plan in place. They continued to make arbitrary hiring decisions based on gut feelings. They didn't know what they were looking for. They eventually lost their funding and their doors closed for good.

The Bureau of Labor Statistics reports that in the year 2000:

- There will be 21 million more job holders and seekers in the United States than in 1986.

- The overall rate of job growth will be approximately 18 percent, which is lower than in previous years.

- The service producing sector will provide 20 million new jobs. Service and retail trade will provide 75 percent of the job growth, and health and business services will account for about half of the growth in services.

- Twenty-three million people now in the labor force are expected to leave. Men are projected to leave in greater numbers than women, by more than 3 million.

- Immigrants will represent the largest share of increase in the U.S. population and work force since World War I.

Will you be prepared for the opportunities that await you? Employees in the 21st century will no doubt place stronger emphasis on employment security, career development and training. It will be more difficult to get entry-level people, and there will be fewer skilled workers from which to choose. To make matters worse, there will be a mismatch between available but unqualified employees. In order to compete in a tight labor market, businesses will have to do a better job of hiring right the first time.

Behavioral Technology®, Inc. estimates the cost of a bad hiring decision for a position paying $25,000 per year as follows:

Cost Factor	Cost Formula: Salary x Estimate of Expense	Amount
Inefficiency/customer costs prior to the person leaving.	$25,000 x 10% of salary	$2,500
Inefficiency/customer costs while a replacement learns the job.	$25,000 x 10% of salary	$2,500
Cost of new hires, recruiting fees, interview travel, etc.	$25,000 x 5% of salary	$1,250
Indirect costs such as low morale loss of customers, abuse of equipment, frustration, etc.	$25,000 x 10% of salary	$2,500
	TOTAL ESTIMATE COST OF A BAD HIRING DECISION	$8,750

Reprinted with written permission of Behavioral Technology®, Inc.

CHAPTER 9

SET THE STAGE

From the initial requisition to interviewing and on-the-job training, the costs of hiring today are extremely high. Expenses include the time spent interviewing and reference checking, agency or search firm fees, relocation packages, medical examination and security clearance expenses, orientation time, an increased learning curve, accounting and payroll expenses, training time or tuition, and this is all before the employee yields any return on the organization's investment.

—Drake Beam Morin, Inc.
Consulting Firm

We probably can all say that at least once in our careers we hired someone who should have never been hired in the first place. That is still no excuse for being ill-prepared to put your best foot forward and live up to your responsibilities as a manager. Employees who move up the organizational ladder into managerial positions are ordained with the power to make hiring decisions, for better or for worse.

In a 1995 survey conducted by The Bureau of National Affairs, Inc. and the Society for Human Resource Management on HR department activities, interviewing was identified in almost two-thirds of the responding organizations (65 percent) as being a shared responsibility with human resource personnel. That means that with over 38 million people working in this country, over one million people will have the responsibility of screening, interviewing and making good hiring decisions in a year's time.

As you prepare for the interview, there are a number of things you can do to make the first few minutes of the interview comfortable for both yourself and the candidate. Think of the process as a team effort or a partnership with the goal of seeing the candidate develop confidence in you. It is only with this type of rapport that the interviewer will get the real story. A harmonious relationship becomes the mechanism that will lead you to the truth concerning the candidate's skills and abilities, strengths and shortcomings. Job candidates will, in many cases, come well-prepared to meet the challenges that await them in the interview. Others will need your encouragement and understanding in order to feel comfortable enough with you to be honest. What you do to prepare for the interview can make the difference between a having worthless conversation and gathering information to help you avoid a bad hiring decision.

T$P # 38: COORDINATE INTERVIEWS

Since there may be several people who will interview each candidate, the job of coordinating the smooth transition from candidate to candidate is generally the responsibility of the human resources department. In smaller organizations the hiring manager may assume this responsibility. In that case, it is important to be sure each candidate is welcomed by the next person to interview them. The interviewer should be using a list of prepared questions and have a complete understanding of what is expected. To avoid too many duplicate questions, you might ask each interviewer to focus on a different area. For example, the Accounting Manager might focus on technical qualifications, while the Operations Manager may be more interested in how well the candidate will interface with those in his or her department. Do a good job of coordinating interviews, and both your managers and the candidates will feel more comfortable and ready to interview.

T$P # 39: NEVER OVER-SCHEDULE

It may be important to identify the best candidate for the job as soon as possible, but interviewing can be exhausting, especially if you schedule one right after the other. Don't over do it and wear yourself out. You don't want to find yourself in a situation whereby you are so sick and tired of interviewing that you do a poor job. You need to be alert and tune into what each candidate is saying. Three to five interviews in one day is plenty, especially if you are successfully gathering versus giving information and documenting your findings.

T$P # 40: EDUCATE ALL HIRING MANAGERS

You may have a good understanding of how to screen, interview and hire, but does everyone else you plan to involve in the process have the same skills? If there is any doubt in your mind, find out what your hiring managers know and don't know. Never allow anyone who does not have full comprehension of the interviewing process and what is expected to participate in interviewing. Not only is there potential legal liability, but you run the risk of not getting the information you need to make a sound hiring decision.

In a large food service organization where turnover was sometimes out of control, managers were not taught how to interview. They simply did what they thought best. In many cases, discriminatory questions were asked which created liabilities almost immediately. In other situations, the managers felt stressed and did a poor job of building rapport and helping the candidate relax. Be sure anyone who is held accountable for hiring gets the necessary training well in advance.

T$P # 41: DETERMINE THE LENGTH OF THE INTERVIEW

Most interviews last 30 minutes to 2 hours. It would be appropriate for a telephone interview to run 30 minutes, as you are trying to get a good feel for the candidate and whether or not you want to schedule a face-to-face interview. However, I have known telephone interviews to last more than 1 hour when the candidate lived out of town, and it was important to the organization not to pay travel expenses for someone who was not a solid candidate. Second and third interviews, as well as interviews with other staff members, could vary depending upon the skill of the interviewer and level of the position.

By following your agenda, you should have little trouble sticking to a schedule, especially when interviewing several candidates. A reasonable amount of time to spend during the first face-to-face interview is 45 to 60 minutes. Some will go longer, and that's OK as long as you are making progress. However, it's to your advantage to know in advance how much time you plan to take for each interview. You can communicate your plan when you begin the interview.

The average one-hour interview would look like this:

*   **Introduction**—includes greeting, small talk,   5 minutes
    introductory statement and opening question.

*   **Work experience**—is most easily obtained by asking   35 minutes
    open and behavior-based questions.

*   **Education**—is easy to discuss and takes only a few   5 minutes
    minutes, unless there is some specific information you need
    to probe.

*   **Answering candidate's questions**—some candidates may   10 minutes
    have questions and others may not, but you should allow time
    for questions.

*   **Summary and closing**—summarize the information you   5 minutes
    have gathered and draw the interview to a close.

Many organizations allow interviews to get totally out of hand in terms of time constraints. They waste hundreds of hours talking to candidates whom they have no interest in hiring. When the interviewer rambles, the candidate often follows suit. Negligence of this nature is robbing organizations of hard-earned money that should be applied to the bottom line.

I generally like my staff to also have the opportunity to interview each candidate. The input of other key employees is important as they will be working closely with whomever is selected. At the end of the interview, you should have all of the information you need to move forward if you've spent most of your time listening and evaluating what you've heard.

T$P # 42: DON'T USE A SUBSTITUTE INTERVIEWER

Never allow a pinch-hitter to conduct the interview for you. All interviews should be done by the hiring manager because he or she is most knowledgeable in exactly what is needed in a candidate and can best determine the match. In organizations where there is a human resource department, they will most likely do the pre-screening. While it is perfectly acceptable for others to interview the candidate later on, the hiring manager should conduct the first interview and not pass off this important responsibility to someone else.

Busy managers frequently delegate interviewing to other people and then wonder why they made the wrong choice. A small company on the West Coast got into the habit of pushing off interviews onto inexperienced managers who had no training in recruiting. Unfortunately, they paid a hefty price when they were sued by a candidate who did not get the job. The candidate said that the interviewer was with him for only 20 minutes during which they talked about "sports." The candidate claimed that he did not get an interview but merely an off-the-cuff conversation with "someone who didn't know how to interview."

The company won the lawsuit but not before shelling out $35,000 in defense costs. In addition to the company being held responsible for the interviewer's actions, the interviewer was personally held liable for what happened. The entire situation was a mess, but the company has changed its strategy to insure nothing like this happens again. Never allow someone else to take your place. Schedule the time and make the commitment that you will handle the interviews for which you are held responsible. Anything less is not acceptable.

T$P # 43: REVIEW DOCUMENTS BEFORE THE INTERVIEW

Fred consistently went into interviews without reading the candidates' resumes, cover letters and/or applications. He stumbled with redundant questions and gave the impression that he was not prepared. Whether due to laziness or poor planning, he allowed his bad habit to create problems. He seldom "connected" with the people he interviewed, and a follow-up survey with those who were actually hired revealed a definite breakdown in communication.

Resumes and/or applications should be reviewed immediately prior to the interview so that the information is fresh in your mind. Nothing is worse than a hiring manager who doesn't know who he or she is interviewing and is redundant in questioning when information is clearly on the resume or application. After reviewing this information, set it aside and get ready with your list of prepared questions.

Decide which behavior-based and open questions would be most appropriate and helpful to you in making your decision. Highlight anything on the resume or application that needs further inquiry and don't be afraid to ask for clarification. This is your chance to find out if the candidate in front of you is up to meeting the challenge you have in mind. If the candidate leaves the interview and you haven't done your job, you have only yourself to blame.

T$P # 44: PREPARE THE SETTING

Not unlike inviting a guest to your home, it is your responsibility to insure that the candidate is interviewed in a comfortable and quiet room behind closed doors. An office is better than a conference room. It's warmer and more inviting because of it's size. As straightforward as this seems, many managers miss the point. You may be comfortable interviewing while sitting on the concrete steps outside your office, or in the breakroom, but the candidate deserves more. Plan ahead and prepare the environment so the candidate feels at home.

Eliminate physical and mental barriers. The days when interviewers positioned themselves in a powerful chair, behind a big desk, are gone. Furniture should be comfortable and arranged so that you and the candidate can face each other without a desk or table separating you. If you can't rearrange the room and find that you must sit behind a desk, place the candidate's chair along side of the desk rather than in front of it. The chairs should be even in height to avoid an impression of superiority over the candidate. Ideally, the chair should have arms for added comfort. You should have an unobstructed view of the candidate, which means nothing should block your sight. Some managers have papers piled high or objects on their desks that limit or even prevent a clear view of the candidate.

Be prepared to offer coffee, tea, a soft drink, or water. This gesture also adds to the comfortable setting. In addition, a beverage helps refresh a candidate whose mouth may become dry from talking or from nervousness. A drink may quench your thirst and clear your throat too.

Never conduct a first interview over a meal. Although the atmosphere may be casual, the interview should be all business. As such, it deserves a business setting. However, a meal may be very appropriate as part of a follow up interview. Meals are excellent forums to help you to see another side of the candidate.

T$P # 45: DON'T TAPE THE INTERVIEW

I am often asked if taping an interview is acceptable. My response to the question is always "no." First, you are violating the law if the candidate is not aware that you are recording. Second, as you recall, one of your goals is to help the candidate feel very comfortable and willing to be open with you. How could anyone possibly feel at ease when being video- or audio-taped during a job interview? Listen carefully and take good notes, and you will get the information you need.

T$P # 46: RECOGNIZE WHAT THE INTERVIEW CAN AND CANNOT MEASURE

Inexperienced hiring managers who expect too much from the interview often find themselves wondering why they didn't get the information they needed to make a sound and defensible hiring decision. Interviews are not the best way to test job skills. These qualifications are better measured by performance tests.

The interview obviously won't prove to you that the candidate can type 75 words per minute, or that the mechanic can repair a transmission on a foreign car, or that a sales manager can sell your product anytime, anywhere. From the interview you won't get a sense of dexterity, speed or the level of quality the candidate strives for. All of these things are best measured with skill tests. What the interview does measure is interpersonal skills and job knowledge, two very important criteria.

The following can be measured in the interview, but it will take practice to understand how to elicit the information to make a decision as to whether or not the candidate has the characteristics as listed:

• Attitude.

• Ability to sell oneself.

• Oral communications skills.

• Personal determination and orientation toward career goals.

- Comprehension.

- Poise, demeanor, social skills, sincerity.

- Ability to analyze information.

Some of this information will be determined by observation. The rest will be decided after questioning candidates through using your list of prepared questions. A recent consulting assignment focused on what an interviewer could learn about the candidate from the interview. I found in talking to the managers that very few of them understood what they could potentially learn from a well-constructed interview. There was a misconception that a handshake, a few words about technical expertise and intuition was enough to know whether or not the candidate was the right fit. They quickly learned what the interview could and could not measure. Today their managers are well on their way to becoming seasoned hiring pros.

T$P # 47: BE ON TIME

Nothing speaks louder than a lack of respect for time. Hiring managers who are late for interviews or keep candidates waiting have done nothing to build rapport. Tardiness sends the message that what is about to take place is not important. If you set an appointment, you are obligated to keep it and be on time. After all, you expect the candidate to reciprocate your punctuality, don't you? Some of you may be thinking, "I know that." You may know it, but are you practicing what you know? We've all heard the old expression, "you only get one chance to make a good first impression." As a hiring manager, you will be leaving the candidate with an impression of you and your organization.

In addition, you should not be tired, distraught or ill-tempered when you interview. I have a colleague who is so grumpy in the morning that anyone who gets in his way feels like they've been run over by a freight train. We've openly talked about his problem and decided that he will never conduct a job interview before 10 A.M. and without a cup or two of coffee in his stomach. He's not an early riser, yet has obligations to meet at work that include interviewing. He's also been known to be late for interviews as much as an hour and a half. Imagine the reaction of the candidates when he comes in late with a bad attitude and no explanation for his tardiness. Fortunately, he's come to terms with his tardiness, which he's always seen as acceptable because he owns the company.

T$P # 48: CONTROL THE INTERVIEW

As the interviewer, you must take charge. You don't want an over-zealous or extremely talkative candidate to take over. If you lose control of the interview, you may run out of time, and you won't have the information you need to make a sound hiring decision. There are several things that you can do to set the stage and insure that the interview stays on track. The interview is not the time to allow rambling and interjection of unrelated information. Yet some hiring managers struggle with the "how to's" of maintaining control especially when meeting up with a talkative candidate. By nature, some candidates will try to control the interview. If you're not assertive and prepared, you may find yourself wasting a lot of time listening to a candidate ramble about something that has nothing to do with the topic at hand.

Some of the most important ways to maintain control of the interview are:

- Share your agenda.

- Review the candidate's qualifications with the candidate to verify your understanding of what is offered.

- Gather versus give information.

- Stick to your list of prepared questions.

- Answer the candidate's questions but only after you have asked all of your questions and are satisfied that you have the information you need to evaluate the candidate.

T$P # 49: APPROACH GROUP INTERVIEWS WITH CAUTION

A group interview is conducted with several people doing the interviewing. This format allows for simultaneous and independent evaluation of candidates while observing the candidate's interactions with other people. Group interviews can be lengthy if all the interviewers have a long list of questions.

Sometimes group interviews takes on a different format. Managers sit around the room and observe a group of candidates as they answer questions that are thrown out to the entire group. Candidates are observed as they interact with each other. Managers watch for signs of aggression as well as timidness. Candidates are under pressure to speak and participate so that they can be evaluated on the things they say to other group members.

Although I am very much in favor of multiple, sequential interviews, I am not particularly in favor of panel or group interviews where a candidate faces a number of people in an almost "firing squad environment." It's sometimes seen as a quick fix, but if not handled well, it is ineffective and can lead to bad hiring decisions. Asking a candidate to sit before a panel of people, all of whom have questions to ask, can be unnerving, one the interviewer should avoid if possible.

If your organization requires you to conduct group or panel interviews, you will want to make an extra special effort to help the candidate feel comfortable. Be sure that you also introduce each group member one-by-one to the candidate in as relaxed of an environment as possible. When candidates are going to be interviewed by a number of people in succession, it's a good idea to ask each interviewer to explore specific issues. One might focus on technical skills, while another checks the candidate's experience in planning and organizing. If you don't assign issues, interviewers don't probe for specific information because they sometimes believe that it has already been done.

T$PS TO REMEMBER

1. Understand that the interview best measures interpersonal skills and job knowledge, not skill level.

2. Read the cover letter, resume and/or application immediately before you meet with the candidate face-to-face for the first time.

3. Allow 45 minutes to 1 hour for the initial interview.

4. Follow an agenda and stick to your questions to avoid getting off track.

5. Be on time for the interview. What is about to take place is very important and deserves your respect.

6. Make sure the interview site is comfortable and inviting. Be prepared to offer a beverage.

7. Don't allow someone else to conduct the interview for you.

8. Rapport is critical to the success of the interview. How you establish and maintain rapport is up to you.

9. Some candidates get very nervous at the thought of a job interview. Put candidates at ease so that they will be honest with you.

10. Never allow interruptions of any kind. It sends the signal that what is taking place is not important.

CHAPTER 10

OPEN THE INTERVIEW

Basically you want to hire someone who is dependable, stable, honest, loyal, responsible, has drive and whose work is valued at equal if not more than their compensation package.

—Dawn Penfold
President of New York-based search firm

How you manage the interview is directly related to what it will cost. If you are effective, you will make a good choice and keep costs to a minimum. If you are not prepared, you will pay the price of a bad hiring decision in a multitude of ways. On average, positions remain vacant for 13 weeks after a bad choice leaves the organization, and an estimated 50 percent of the position's efficiency is sacrificed during that time. Controlling the costs of a bad hiring decision is one of the most effective ways to impact the bottom line in your organization. You can become a valuable contributor to the corporate balance sheet by hiring good employees the first time. The loss of an employee due to a bad decision goes beyond losing the productivity of one person. There are administrative expenses and indirect costs to the organization, including diminished productivity in the weeks before the employee leaves. Increased workloads and the disruption in operational flow among the employees who are left and must pick up the slack, reduces the effectiveness of everyone.

Many things go into managing the interview, the most critical part of the hiring process. From asking permission to take notes to formal documentation of your findings, all of your actions contribute to the success or failure of the interview, which requires a plan, discipline and motivation to find the best people available. Hiring the right people makes the job of training, motivating, managing, and evaluating much easier. Recruiting and selecting is a vital function of your job as a manager. The effort that you put into developing your leadership abilities in this area will pay dividends for years to come.

Making the right choice is directly related to getting your costs under control for several reasons:

- The right choice, who has the skills needed to do the job, is immediately more productive than someone who does not meet the job requirements.

- The right choice needs less supervisory time.

- The right choice is satisfied with the new job and eager to learn and make a contribution, which means less risk that the person will leave.

- The right choice does not hurt the morale in an organization but actually helps maintain good morale.

- The right choice comes to work every day, unlike the wrong choice who may become an absentee problem.

- The right choice is a contributor to the growth and success of the organization, while the bad choice is a drain on the energy and productivity of everyone with whom they come in contact.

The symptoms of a bad hiring decision are closely associated with turnover. Unhappy employees who were not the right choice from the beginning often create problems within the organization. At first their dissatisfaction may be subtle, but gradually it escalates until you have no alternative but to confront the problem if it has not already been addressed. Sometimes the employee elects to leave the organization; sometimes you make the decision to terminate the relationship. You are the gatekeeper and have the power to prevent an interview from becoming a new hire disaster.

Some hiring managers make the right decision for the short term, but many fail to think ahead about how the final choice will fit into the organization. According to the American Society for Training and Development, when a senior employee leaves, it costs an organization an estimated one-and-a-half times his or her salary or more. This figure represents the high cost in time as well as money of training a successor as well as recruiting costs and the impact of morale on the rest of the organization. The average cost of an entry-level employee who is a bad choice is $6,000. How to stop bad hiring decisions from getting out of control has a lot to do with how you manage the interview.

T$P # 50: GREET THE CANDIDATE

How you greet the candidate is the beginning of a relationship, not just an interview. The first encounter is the foundation for success, so don't send your secretary or someone else to the reception area to greet the candidate and bring the individual to your office. This important task should be yours alone.

Ben was a laissez-faire manager who never greeted candidates in person. He could see them on his video screen in his office. He could talk with them on a speaker phone that was located in the company's lobby and "buzz" them through the front security door without ever having to get out of his chair. He would give the candidates directions to his office that was located in the back of an enormous building and pour himself a cup of coffee while he waited the five minutes it took for the individuals to navigate through the long hallways on the way to see him. Obviously, there were a number of problems with what he was doing, including security and safety issues. Can you imagine how candidates reacted when they heard his voice over an intercom telling them to "follow the yellow brick road," which was actually "bricks" painted onto a cement walkway that zigged-zagged throughout the main areas of the company? By the time the candidates found his office, many were anxious and uncomfortable as they greeted an imposing interviewer sitting behind an enormous oak desk.

To ease the anxiety for the candidate associated with meeting you and being interviewed, you can prepare to greet candidates, as follows:

- **Call the candidates by name.** It immediately personalizes the conversation and makes the candidates feel good upon hearing their own names, especially when used by the hiring manager in greeting the candidate.

- **Offer a firm handshake.** This positive gesture communicates in a non-verbal manner your acceptance of the individual.

- **Smile.** Nothing compares to the power of a smile, whether acknowledging a stranger or meeting the candidate for the first time. Most of us do not smile enough, a tool that can do a lot to build instant rapport and improve how we look by 100 percent.

These actions send the message that you feel the candidate is important and that you have been looking forward to your meeting. Hiring managers sometimes fall short in this area. Your message through your initial greeting needs to say loud and clear that nothing is more important than the candidate and the time you will spend together in the interview.

T$P # 51: ESTABLISH RAPPORT

A proper greeting opens the door to good rapport, but you can do more to help the candidate relax. Easing your way toward a comfortable connection with the candidate should be your first objective immediately prior to beginning the interview. Think of the job interview as building a relationship that can have a major impact on whether or not the candidate will feel comfortable enough with you to be honest and open. Be sensitive to your eye contact and body language, all of which send subtle messages. Make sure your communication on all levels is one of sincere interest and warmth. Try not to prejudge candidates in the first few seconds, but instead give them the benefit of the doubt. They may be hesitant to speak up and a bit intimidated by the interview process. Help them get started, and you will find that your sensitivity to their needs will reap its rewards as candidates open up to you.

It takes time to build rapport. If you don't get it from the start or lose it during the interview, you've lost valuable time, and time is money. It takes about 11 minutes to build rapport in the average interview. If you spend this amount of time building rapport and lose it, it will take you another 8 minutes to re-establish rapport and in some cases, you will never regain it once lost.

T$P # 52: PUT NERVOUS CANDIDATES AT EASE

Not surprisingly, many people are nervous during job interviews. It's the hiring manager's responsibility to help candidates relax, who are usually nervous because they have not interviewed in a long time. Perhaps, they had a bad experience in the past, or maybe the candidate needs the job so bad that he or she is almost paralyzed during the interview. There is also the possibility that candidates are not fluent in English and feel uncomfortable speaking their second language. Whatever the reason, putting candidates at ease is important if you are going to get to know them. We've all had to look for a job at one time or another. Don't ever lose sight of what that experience was like. It can be, as you may recall, a very difficult time in your life.

I've interviewed many nervous candidates during my career, but one stands out in my mind. She was so nervous she cried during the interview and I later found out that she got sick in the lobby on her way out the door. She was a mother who was returning to the work force after raising five children and going through a violent divorce. A bright woman with low self-esteem, I called her back for a second interview and later offered her the job. She was stunned. Her willingness to learn and basic intelligence had a lot to do with my decision along with the fact that she met my job requirements. She recently passed her 15-year anniversary with the company, has earned a two-year degree in accounting and was promoted from the warehouse into the office.

If you find yourself in a complicated or difficult situation with a candidate like this one, think about how you would want to be treated. Helping the candidate feel at ease is a very important responsibility that should never be taken for granted.

T$P # 53: SHARE YOUR AGENDA

After you've greeted the candidate and as you are building rapport, it would be appropriate to discuss how you plan to proceed in the interview. You might say something like, "I'd like to spend about one hour with you. I'll begin by asking you a series of questions, the same questions that I am asking each of the candidates. I want you to feel comfortable. When I am finished, I'd like you to feel free to ask me anything you wish. How does that sound?"

By sharing your agenda, you are not only letting the candidate know that you are organized, but your are making it clear in a pleasant way that you have a time schedule to follow. A system will keep the interview at a professional level and prevent the conversation from getting out of control or an answer from going off on a tangent. An agenda sets the stage for a well-managed interview.

T$P # 54: ASK PERMISSION TO TAKE NOTES

If you feel you must take notes and are not proficient at making accurate notes after the interview, always ask permission to do so. However, don't take notes to the point that you lose eye contact and rapport. Jotting down a few words to help you later recall what was discussed is perfectly acceptable and will help you remember points that are especially important. By asking permission, the candidate will feel comfortable; the more you do to help the candidate relax, the more effective you will be in the interview. I generally say something like, "Do you mind if I take a few notes while we talk? I want to be sure I capture the highlights of your career." At the end of the interview I may even review my notes orally with the candidate to verify what I have written in my notes is actually what the candidate said.

Put yourself in the candidate's place. Have you ever been in a situation where you were interviewed and suddenly the interviewer started feverishly taking notes as you spoke? Or have you ever felt uncomfortable in a doctor's office when the nurse took your case history? Were you the least bit curious when the doctor added to what she had written? Have you ever wondered if what was written about you in an interview or doctor's office was a precise description of what you thought you said?

To have an accurate record of the interview while also making the candidate feel at ease, I highly recommend that you ask permission to take notes. Don't get yourself in a situation like a manager I know who interviewed 15 candidates in rapid succession for three different positions. She never took notes because she felt it would make the candidates uncomfortable. As a result, she had nothing to refer back to, and thus was very confused about who said what. After some coaching, she became very good at asking permission to take notes immediately after pleasantries were exchanged. To this day no one has ever said to her, "No, I don't want you to take notes during the interview." Instead, she receives overwhelming acceptance from each candidate she asks and later has notes to refer back to after each interview.

T$P # 55: ELIMINATE INTERRUPTIONS

If you want to maximize the benefits of the interview, you must provide a degree of privacy. Hold telephone calls and eliminate interruptions of all kinds, even if you have to leave the building to conduct the interview. Disruptions during the interview caused by others bursting into the room or by ringing telephones reflect negatively on you and the company.

Many years ago I was interviewed for a job by someone who knew nothing about building rapport. The interviewer permitted a half-a-dozen telephone interruptions and allowed the secretary to interrupt three times. All of this took place within 60 minutes. No rapport was ever established. The entire event was a sad commentary on the interviewer's lack of professionalism. I see this happen a lot. Unfortunately, busy managers feel that some things can't wait and that it's OK to stop the interview to answer a question or take a phone call. In the long run, you lose the momentum that could make the difference between getting enough information to make a good decision and getting so little information that no decision can be made.

T$P # 56: BE CONSISTENT IN QUESTIONING

Each candidate should be asked the same questions from your prepared list. Always focus on qualifications for the job. It's much easier to compare candidates if you are measuring everyone against the same criteria. If you develop your questions ahead of time, based on the information you need to know, you will feel very comfortable in questioning. Although you will probe for additional information based on individual responses, you will still ask each candidate the same questions.

In preparing for a retained search, I developed a list of questions that would elicit the kind of information needed to make an informed decision about each candidate. Comparing candidates became easy as each responded differently to the same situation. When asking behavior-based questions, it was especially helpful to find out how each candidate would respond to the same question. There was a large variance in their answers. I was the only one who knew what kind of response I needed to hear in order to promote the candidate to the next level of the hiring process.

One candidate had an interesting response to the question, "Can you tell me about a time when you fired someone?" He perked up in his chair and a glow came over his face as he proudly revealed that he had fired dozens of people during his career, probably over one hundred. He said something like, "You win some and you lose some." As the interviewer, I knew immediately that his response to that question was not what I wanted to hear. The person to be hired was to take over a staff, all of whom were afraid that the new president would bring his or her own people into the company and terminate the existing staff. The last thing my client needed was someone who took pleasure in ruining people's lives.

T$P # 57: AVOID REDUNDANT QUESTIONS

Don't waste your time asking questions to which the answer is already provided on the resume or application. The questions you ask should be for additional information or to probe deeper. When you ask redundant questions, you not only look incompetent, but it's very annoying to the candidate.

Here are some examples of the right and wrong way to ask a question based on the information you have in front of you:

- "You worked at ABC Company from 1979–1991, is that correct?" **A better question would be:** "I see that you worked at ABC Company for 13 years. Why did you decide to change jobs in 1991?"

  With the second question you not only verify that the candidate was employed during the time indicated on the resume, but you ask for additional information with your second question.

OR

• "I see that you are a journeyman tool and die maker. Have you done that kind of work most of your life?" It should be obvious from the resume that the candidate either has worked in the field most of his life or has not.

A better question would be: "I see you are a journeyman tool and die maker. What is the most challenging part of your job? If you could do it over, would you choose the same line of work? Why or why not?"

The second question gets more information and opens the door for the candidate to speak to you about what interests him or her and the reason behind a specific career choice.

Anything you ask should help you gather additional information that goes beyond what you already know or what appears on the resume or application. This is another reason you need to plan ahead and work from your list of prepared questions.

T$P # 58: ASK ONLY JOB-RELATED QUESTIONS

Employment application forms and pre-employment interviews have traditionally been instruments for eliminating at an early stage "unsuited" or "unqualified" people from consideration for employment and often have been used in such a way as to restrict or deny employment opportunities for women and minorities.

The law, interpreted through court rulings and EEOC decisions, prohibits the use of all pre-employment inquiries and qualifying factors that disproportionately screen out members of minority groups or members of one sex and are not valid predictors of successful job performance or cannot be justified by "business necessity."

In developing or reviewing application forms or in seeking informa-tion from job applicants, employers should ask themselves the following questions:

- Will the answer to this question, if used in making a selection, have a "disparate effect" in screening out minorities and/or members of one sex (i.e., disqualify a significantly larger per-centage of members of a particular group over others)?

- Is this information really needed to judge an applicant's compe-tence or qualification for the job in question?

The concept of "business necessity" has been narrowly defined by the courts. When a practice is found to have discriminatory effects, it can be justified only by showing that it is necessary to the safe and efficient operation of the business, that it effectively carries out the purpose it is supposed to serve and that there are no alternative policies or practices which would better or equally well serve the same purpose with less discriminatory impact.

As an employer, you should be able to demonstrate through statisti-cal evidence that any selection procedure which has a "disparate effect" on groups protected by the law is job-related, (i.e., validity predicts successful performance in the type of job in question). If this cannot be shown or if you as the employer cannot or do not wish to perform a technical validation study, the use of that procedure should be discontin-ued or altered in such a way that there is no longer a discriminatory effect. Even when a procedure having an adverse impact can be validated, it may not be used if there are other procedures which would accomplish the same goal and have less of a discriminatory effect (from the EEOC's *Guide to Pre-Employment Inquiries* as published by The Bureau of National Affairs, Inc.)

Interviewers who ask personal questions or questions that are not job-related run the risk of being charged with discrimination. Here is a sample of what you may not ask:

- How old are you; what is your date of birth?

- Are you married?

- How tall are you? How much do you weigh?

- Have you ever been arrested?

- Does your religion prevent you from working weekends or holidays?

- Do you rent or own your home?

- Are you disabled?

All of these questions are in violation of EEO guidelines. You may not ask these questions under any circumstances. Appendix B provides additional information on acceptable and discriminatory questions.

T$P # 59: TREAT CANDIDATES LIKE YOUR BEST CUSTOMERS

The interview is a great opportunity to put your best foot forward by treating each and every candidate like your very best customer. Roll out the red carpet and be prepared to show your candidates how important they are. From the minute they walk into your organization, they should get the royal treatment. Who knows, if they don't get the job, they still could end up being your best customer some day.

Some employers do a better job than others in this area, but one organization I know does an exceptionally good job. The company makes a real effort to show candidates that they are a people-oriented business. From greeting to closing the interview, they focus on turning an interview into a relationship. At the end of the interview, each candidate receives a gift box of their products, exactly like one which is given to new customers. It's a nice gesture that while it costs the company a few dollars, generates goodwill that in their mind is worth the price.

T$P # 60: RECOGNIZE DIVERSITY AS A PLUS

With a rapidly changing population you will see more candidates with diverse backgrounds, more women, more disadvantaged, more people for whom English is their second language and fewer white males. Differences in cultural heritage go hand-in-hand with types and levels of experience and education as well as dress and appearance. There's no doubt that the U.S. workforce will continue to become more diverse as time passes.

Progressive leaders are looking for ways to integrate diversity into the organization and take advantage of the mix of talent and differences these groups bring with them. In some cases, diversity may present barriers in terms of speaking, reading and writing English; however, there are usually job opportunities within most organizations that may not require a high level of sophistication in language skills in order to meet the other job requirements. Don't overlook this potential resource; don't think of diversity as a disadvantage, when in reality, there are many advantages to a diverse group of people working together as a team.

T$PS TO REMEMBER

1. Never delegate to others the important task of greeting a candidate.

2. Establish rapport within the first few minutes of the interview.

3. Share your agenda and ask permission to take notes.

4. Don't allow interruptions. To do so sends the signal that the interview is not important.

5. Consistency in questions will also help you avoid redundancy.

6. Stay out of court by asking job-related questions only.

7. Diversity can bring an exciting new dimension to your business. Make an effort to recognize and recruit a diverse work force.

CHAPTER 11

FINE TUNE YOUR SKILLS

Innocent questions often result in companies having to defend against costly and time-consuming charges of discrimination filed with the federal EEOC and various state agencies, including the Human Rights Commission and the Attorney General's Office. If discrimination is found, an applicant may be awarded damages including a job offer, attorney costs and other benefits.

—Steven Mitchell Sack
Attorney

Your job as a manager is undergoing a major shift in the way screening, interviewing and hiring is being approached. With re-engineering of the work force, thousands of candidates with varying degrees of skills have flooded the job market. Are you in a position to upgrade the skills of an individual who was a bad hiring decision or would it be more cost-effective to devote your energy to fine tuning your interviewing skills and increasing the probability that you will hire right the first time? Many experts agree that as a country, we have under-invested in skills development of managers and supervisors. Although some managers may have a "knack" for selecting the best people, everyone is not blessed with this natural ability. Good hiring decisions go beyond intuition because gut feelings are often misleading. It doesn't mean you should ignore your instincts, but they should be substantiated with facts that can only be obtained by sharpening your interviewing skills.

What protects you from the professional job seeker who shines in the interview, but tarnishes quickly once employed? Perhaps you have a "mental yardstick" that will help you sort out the winners from the losers. It all goes back to skills versus intuition. With hiring costs at 30 percent of the annual salary to replace an entry-level employee and an estimated replacement cost of five times the annual salary for executives, it's not surprising that employers everywhere are taking a more critical look at their hiring practices.

You can increase your chances for finding the perfect match by refining your interviewing skills. Since most candidates have stock answers for interview questions, you will need to ask some less typical questions. How far are you willing to go to insure that you make the right hiring decision the first time?

T$P # 61: ACTIVELY LISTEN

The energy you put into the interview will reap its rewards. Pay attention to what the candidate is saying and don't let your mind wander. The physical environment can make a difference in your ability to tune in and listen. If the room is too warm or too cold, you cannot possibly devote your full attention to understanding what the candidate says. If you are not a good listener, practice developing the skill.

The best way to communicate with the candidate that you are listening to is an occasional nod of the head, good eye contact, and an "uh huh" or "yes." Facial expressions also indicate understanding, as well as your attentiveness and overall body language. Your signals that you're listening are important.

During the interview, you will want to listen specifically for:

- Areas that the candidate appears to want to avoid discussing.

- Statements that are general rather than specific.

- Information that the candidate volunteers or seems to want to discuss.

- Silence, long pauses, hesitation.

• Anything you suspect might not be truthful.

• Weaknesses revealed by the candidate.

The 80/20 rule is one to keep in mind. Listen 80 percent of the time and speak 20 percent of the time. Talking too much is undoubtedly one of the biggest mistakes hiring managers make. Whether anxious about the task ahead or anxious to talk about themselves, managers not allowing the candidate to do most of the talking is a common but avoidable mistake.

T$P # 62: WATCH FOR NON-VERBAL CUES

The spoken word as well as non-verbal communication cues can help you learn about the candidate. Most people agree that they can do a much better job of listening. Facial expressions and eye contact communicate agreement, understanding, confusion, questions, surprise, fear, and more. Body language also communicates emotion. Not only will you be "listening" for non-verbal cues from candidates, you will also be communicating with them through your face and body language.

In an article entitled "The Messages of Body Language in Job Interviews" by Scott T. Fleischmann, which appeared in *Employment Relations Today*, Summer 1991, he discusses how the careful observation and interpretation of body language is a tool every interviewer and hiring manager should be familiar with. He describes the job of the interviewer as noting the characteristics that are consistent with the candidate's statements and probing those areas that are not. For example, everyone has a breathing pattern that is most comfortable. Nervousness, frustration, confusion, and stress change the pattern. Toward the end of the rapport-building segment of the interview, the candidate should be breathing in a pattern that is comfortable. Unless the person shows other signs of being abnormally nervous, the interviewer can use this pattern as a baseline. If the breathing becomes short and more shallow as the interview progresses, the candidate is probably frustrated or anxious, says Fleischmann. In this case, more probing is in order.

In *Eye to Eye—How People React* by Peter Marsh, the author's research substantiates the fact that the eyes are the most expressive part of the face and offer clues to what the candidate is thinking. For example, narrowing the eyes may indicate disagreement, resentment, anger, or disapproval.

Raised eyebrows indicate surprise, and peering over the top of the glasses can be a sign of doubt or disbelief. Hand and arm motions can show almost as much expression as the face. There's no doubt that people use their bodies to communicate, and only interviewers who are prepared to tune in to this language will benefit from what is being said without words.

If you feel a need to improve your non-verbal communication, there are several steps you can take:

• Find out what you look like to others by video taping yourself in a mock interview.

• Identify your nervous or bad habits such as biting your lip, pulling on your ear, sniffing, clearing your throat, scratching your head, pushing your eyeglasses up onto the bridge of your nose, etc. Concentrate on not doing the things that others may see as annoying or distracting.

• Exercise your facial muscles by smiling as long as it doesn't look phony.

• Be aware of gestures, especially crossing your arms and legs, which tend to indicate that you are not open to new ideas.

T$P # 63: HEAR WHAT THE CANDIDATE IS *NOT* SAYING

Sometimes what the candidate does not say can be just as revealing as what is said. For example, a candidate who eagerly discusses work experience but appears to intentionally avoid discussing one particular previous employer could have something to hide. Another example might be a candidate who, when asked how he or she got along with a previous supervisor, avoids answering the question by talking about other successful working relationships. If you can "hear" what is not being said, it will give you some additional insight into the candidate if you probe for more information and better understanding.

I've interviewed thousands of candidates over the last twenty years, but none was more memorable than an executive level candidate who's answers to my questions were so evasive that I learned almost nothing about him during the interview. I used every technique I could think of to get him to open up. On paper he appeared to be very qualified but seemed uncomfortable as we talked. Finally, I asked him if something was wrong. Looking rather sheepish, he told me there was something about him that I should know. He went on to tell me that he was a nudist and hoped I wouldn't hold it against him!

I thought something was going on, but never dreamed that what I was hearing he was *not* saying was that he didn't know how to tell me he was hiding something he thought was important. Evidently, he was very active in his nudist community and felt that I, as well as others in the organization, would eventually find out about his lifestyle if he was hired. He didn't know how to broach the subject in the interview, so he brought a lot of suspicion down on himself through what he didn't say.

T$P # 64: USE THE "ECHO" TECHNIQUE

This technique will allow you to gather additional information that might not come out otherwise. Repeat a word or phrase from an answer just given by the candidate and add an inflection at the end. Your "echo" encourages the candidate to tell you more. An example of how to use the "echo" technique, with myself as the interviewer, might sound something like this:

Example:

Candidate: "The hours I worked on my last job sometimes stressed me out."

Interviewer: "Stressed you out?"

Candidate: "Yes, I worked so many hours that I felt like my job owned me. I was very unhappy."

Interviewer: "You felt your job owned you; can you be more specific?"

Candidate: "I started work at 8 P.M. and sometimes didn't leave until 6 P.M. It was really getting to me. I felt like I had no time for myself."

Interviewer: "Long hours can be stressful."

Candidate: "It's just not what I want. What kind of hours would I have to work here?

At that point, I thought about the long hours our employees worked. It wasn't uncommon for people to start at 7 A.M. and wrap it up after 7 P.M. if we had orders to get out. Our employees were also required to work every other Saturday from 6 A.M. to 3 P.M. Based on what I learned about the candidate through my use of the "echo" technique, I knew that he would not be happy in the organization.

Don't get me wrong, I know 7 A.M. to 7 P.M. is a long day and that requiring people to work every other Saturday can be a burden, but it was made clear during the interview that these were the expectations. During the slow season in July and December the company closes for one week. They also have a generous compensation policy in that they pay employees for each of the two weeks they are closed, in addition to their regular paid vacation.

T$P # 65: DON'T RUSH THE CANDIDATE FOR A RESPONSE

Never rush the candidate after asking a question. Allow candidates time to collect their thoughts and in their minds compose their best answers. You don't ever want to start firing questions one right after the other. Relax and give candidates a chance to respond. If you personally are short on time, you should not have scheduled the interview to begin with, but waited until you had an hour to devote your full attention to the interview.

I've coached many managers on how to improve their interviewing skills. I've seen interviewers race through an interview appearing to be focused only on putting it behind them. I've seen other managers who don't make the time they set aside for the interview a priority. As a result, the candidates are shortchanged by not getting a fair shot at selling themselves, and the interviewer loses the opportunity to hear a candidate's best response to the question asked. It's just plain rude to put pressure on a candidate to respond quickly.

T$P # 66: PROBE FOR UNDERSTANDING

Accepting what the candidate says at face value without questioning further the reasons behind the statement can lead to a bad hiring decision, which often means lower productivity, lost customers and the stress of having to manage a bad choice. Interviewers are sometimes afraid that they might be invading the candidate's privacy and that can be a valid concern. However, when a candidate says for example, in response to your question, "I quit my job because I didn't get along with my supervisor," you have a right to find out more about what the candidate means by that statement. Did the candidate really quit, or was he or she terminated? What does the candidate mean by "didn't get along with my supervisor?" What was the degree of conflict? Did it ever get physical; was it verbal confrontation or did the candidate suffer in silence?

You have a right as a hiring manager to probe for clarification and understanding. You may even want to telephone the candidate after the interview to gather additional information or clarify something that is questionable in your mind. If at all possible, don't allow the interview to end without having obtained the information you need to make a decision concerning your level of interest in the candidate.

T$P # 67: DON'T BE FOOLED BY THE "HALO EFFECT"

The "halo effect" is one of many sources of error that an interviewer faces that threatens the validity, reliability and legality of the interviewing process. Along with social stereotypes, indiscriminate use of hunches and inaccurate documentation and ranking, the "halo effect," is something that hiring managers must be aware of if they want to avoid problems down the road.

A form of bias, the "halo effect" tends to judge someone favorably in many areas on the basis of one strong point on which the interviewer places high value or has something in common. For example, the interviewer who places high value on organizational skills may judge candidates who appear to be well-organized to have many other favorable qualities that they may not have. Unfortunately, these assumptions may or may not be true, but even if they are, it still doesn't mean the candidate is the best choice for the job. Just being aware that the "halo effect" exists will help managers avoid bad hiring decisions.

T$P # 68: RECOGNIZE THE "HORNS EFFECT"

The opposite of the "halo effect," the interviewer is influenced by something negative and fails to evaluate the positives. For example, the candidate has a dialect, and the interviewer feels that everyone with such a dialect acts in a certain way. The interviewer allows what is perceived as a negative to overshadow the positives, and thus good candidates are never seriously considered. I know a woman who was not considered for a position because she was overweight. I tried to convince the hiring manager, not only that he was discriminatory in his actions, but that she was more qualified than all of the other candidates combined. My attempts were unsuccessful as he let the "horns effect" cloud his thinking. He assumed that because she was overweight, she lacked the qualities needed to do the job. He gave up the opportunity to hire the best employee he could have ever had. Shortly thereafter, I hired her for myself!

T$P # 69: GATHER VERSUS GIVE INFORMATION

Sometimes we are so excited about the organization, the job and the opportunity that we say too much too early in the interview. The interview is your chance to gather as much information as you can about the candidate by asking questions and listening. You can't listen when you are talking. In addition, when you give too much information, you "color" or influence what you get back.

Candidates have every right to put their best foot forward, and many are very experienced at interviewing. A sharp candidate will listen carefully and respond to your questions by telling you what you want to hear. The best way to prevent yourself from giving too much information is by telling the candidate that you would like to ask a number of questions and when you are finished, you will be happy to answer any questions he or she may have. In other words, stick to your plan.

If you don't begin the interview by explaining what your agenda is and how you would like to proceed, you give the candidate the opportunity to interrupt you by asking questions before you have had a chance to gather the information you need to make an informed decision. Savvy candidates may even throw your first question back to you by asking you to tell them more about the organization and the job before they answer your question. Inexperienced hiring managers sometimes talk incessantly. Before they know it, they have rambled on for 30 minutes and told the candidate everything that he or she needs to know in order to successfully sell themselves, including the kind of person envisioned for the position.

My own experience as a job seeker comes to mind when I think about the number of inexperienced interviewers I have encountered over the years. I met a charming man in a job interview who devoted 40 minutes to telling me about the company, the job and the ideal candidate. I questioned him; I probed for more information about what he was looking for. I got the job offer. Need I say more?

T$P # 70: DETERMINE WEAKNESSES

One of the most important responsibilities you have as an interviewer is to get a good feel for the candidate's skills and experience as well as determine weaknesses. If you know the candidate's weaknesses, you are in a better position to decide whether or not to hire someone. You can determine weaknesses through open questions. You can also ask candidates what they see as their weaknesses. You will find that many answer honestly, partly due to the level of rapport you have built with them from the start of the interview. Others will have a canned answer to your question; however, don't accept it if you really want to know about deficiencies. In asking about weaknesses, I usually say something like, "We all have things we are working on to improve or become better at in what we do. Can you share with me three areas that you are focusing on for improvement?" Once you've asked the question, listen carefully as the answers will be very revealing.

Another approach to finding out about weaknesses is through a series of questions. For example, if you wanted to find out about or had some doubt about the candidate's ability or willingness to work as a team player, you might ask questions like this:

- "Can you tell me about a time on your last job when you had a conflict with a peer?"

- "How do you manage to work with someone who regularly disagrees with your point of view?"

- "Can you tell me about a time when you had to do a job and work with people you didn't like?"

All three of these questions will help you get information on strengths, but more importantly, weaknesses of the candidates. These questions are behavior-based and ask the individual to describe something that actually took place. When listening to the answer, you will get a good picture of how the candidate has reacted in the past. Past behavior is a reliable indicator of the future.

The most important relationship in any job situation is that between the supervisor and the employee. It is imperative that you discover through the interview process the "real person." If you recognize the weaknesses, you can make a decision. You will either not be willing to accept the candidate as is, or will be willing to live with the weaknesses (we all have them) and help with overcoming those that will potentially impact the job performance.

T$P # 71:   PROVIDE ONLY A REALISTIC PICTURE OF THE JOB

When candidates are in short supply, it is sometimes tempting to paint an untrue or overly complimentary picture of the job. However, once on the payroll, if the picture begins to fade, you will have a disappointed employee on your hands. Misleading the candidate during the interview is not only unethical but could lead to legal problems. You are better off being honest from the beginning about the work, hours and anything else that will impact the decision of the candidate.

Hiring managers who promise or imply certain benefits or monetary rewards both in base salary and commissions or bonuses, whether in an attempt to get the candidate to join their organization or just to boast about what they can offer, invite trouble later when the candidate discovers you broke your "promises."

The Federal Trade Commission considers statements that promise earnings which exceed the average net earnings of your other employees in the case of sales positions to be unfair and deceptive trade practices. The candidates can actually ask to see wage statements of other sales people in your organization to prove your claims. Overselling the job can become a major liability as can promises of job security. Lawsuits against ex-employers are filed more often than ever before by former employees who claim breach of oral agreements promising job security. A jury in

Michigan recently awarded $1.1 million to a former employee based on an oral "promise" of lifetime employment.

A case that went to court several years ago was won by a managerial level candidate who was able to prove after being hired that the job which was described in the interview was not the job she got. The interviewer had promised her a secretary, her own office with a "view," a high degree of independence, three weeks of vacation, and her first performance review three months from the day she started.

Instead, she got no clerical support and had to type her own correspondence on an obsolete computer. She had to walk to another floor to a printer. Her office with a "view" was an open cubicle that faced the noisy break room and looked out over a trash-strewn courtyard. She was supervised closely by her boss who acted like a drill sergeant. She was told after she started she would get three weeks of vacation but not until she had been employed there five years. When she wanted to leave, she was persuaded by her manager to stay. She was later fired and she sued. The courts ruled in her favor.

T$P # 72: DON'T MAKE MORAL JUDGEMENTS

Never put the candidate in the position of having to take a defensive posture by asking questions that may be perceived as judgmental. All questions should be open and positive in nature. Many things can potentially be revealed during the interview. As a hiring manager you have no business making comments concerning the candidate's lifestyle, financial position, sexual preference, etc. Your decision to hire should be based totally on whether or not the candidate meets your job requirements. Getting on a soap box to further your own interests or express your opinions is something that should never take place during the interview.

An individual who was responsible for interviewing and hiring people for his department was sued by a candidate who was able to prove the questions the interviewer asked that were related to her religious convictions were inappropriate. The hiring manager, who was a devote Christian, probed a candidate until she admitted she was an atheist. The manager then used the interview to try to convert the woman or at least get her to consider rejoining a church. The moral judgment he imposed upon her and the discussion that followed was illegal.

T$P # 73: FIND OUT IF THE CANDIDATE CAN DO WHAT IS CLAIMED

Find out if the candidate can do what is claimed, and you will have a valuable piece of information. How you go about finding out may be easier than you think. Simply ask candidates to tell you in as much detail as they can what one would have to do in order to, for example, prepare a budget, or organize a staff meeting, or repair a transmission, or discipline an employee, etc. If the individual has actually done what is claimed, it can be explained. Anyone who cannot provide the specifics to back up a claim should be considered questionable. With additional follow up questions, you can satisfy any concerns you may have.

A sample conversation regarding whether or not the candidate knows as claimed, how to complete a sales ticket when merchandise is sold in a retail store might sound like this:

Interviewer: "Please tell me in as much detail as you can what steps you take in completing a sales ticket when you sell a washer, dryer, refrigerator, or other major appliance in your current job."

Candidate: "First, I write in the customer's name, address, city, state, zip code, and home and business telephone numbers under 'purchased by'."

"Next, I complete the information on where the item or items is to be delivered, which may be different from the customer's address."

"If it's an apartment or condominium, I include the complex name."

"I record the store number and my name and my sales associate number."

"I record the method of payment—cash, check or charge—along with the name of the credit card if appropriate."

"I record the stock number of the item."

"I write a description of the item."

"I code how the item will get to the customer, i.e., we deliver, customer picks up, we ship, etc."

"I record the retail price and if there is a discount or sale price I enter that information on the form."

"I record the total price including tax and delivery charges."

"I record charge for setup if applicable."

As you can see by the detailed information the candidate was able to provide, she was experienced in completing documentation on the sale of merchandise. You can tell by listening to her that she knows what she is talking about. Although what you require in your store may be slightly different from the procedure she is familiar with, you know that she has done what she claims she can do.

T$P # 74: GET COMFORTABLE WITH SILENCE

An awkward pause or period of silence should not be viewed as a time to jump in and speak for the candidate. Sometimes interviewers feel uncomfortable during moments of silence. In actuality, it's a good time to collect your thoughts and allow the candidate to reflect on what's been said. There's no need to feel that someone must be talking at all times. In addition, silence indicates to the candidate that you are looking for more information. And the more information you get the easier it will be to make an informed hiring decision.

Elizabeth is a manager who is very uncomfortable with silence and tends to break the silence by quickly moving onto other questions. By doing so, candidates get off the hook on tough questions, and Elizabeth does not get the information she needs. In an effort to improve her interviewing skills, she made a commitment to herself to hold back from putting words in the mouths of her candidates or jumping in with small talk to fill the void. She is not perfect yet, but has made a big improvement in how she handles awkward pauses during the interview.

T$P # 75: DON'T LET YOUR BODY LANGUAGE REVEAL YOUR THOUGHTS

Just because we are human, sometimes we express how we really feel about something or someone by the expression on our face, our tone of voice or through our gestures. By showing too much approval, you communicate that you like what the candidate is saying. You are sending the message that he or she is on the right tract. On the other hand, if you subtly say you disapprove of something that was said, the candidate may clam up or say things to try to impress you that isn't a true reflection of character.

Telegraphing candidates with either the fact that you are excited about them and the things they are telling you and plan to make a job offer or that you are dissatisfied with what you are hearing leads to bad hiring decisions. Be pleasant and do the things necessary to conduct an effective interview, but keep your reactions to yourself.

T$P # 76: AVOID STRESS TACTICS

Attacking a candidate during the interview or applying undue pressure rarely yields meaningful information. You have merely created a hypothetical situation that may be very unlike the real thing. There is nothing to support the theory that stress interviews reveal an individual's ability to handle pressure in a real-life situation. Some hiring managers believe that by using stress tactics such as pointing out weaknesses, constantly interrupting and not allowing candidates to finish what they were saying is the best way to test ability to handle stress. Other managers intimidate by showing they have more knowledge, continually disagreeing with candidates or are rude, belligerent or antagonistic. They want to see if the candidate will become flustered, angry or lose control.

Some managers have intentionally seated candidates in a squeaky or wobbly chair, next to a loud fan or in a spot where sun glares into the candidate's eyes. All of these tactics are a sign of a poor interviewer. People are always more willing to discuss their liabilities when assured that they have gained someone's respect. Learn how a candidate manages stress through a series of carefully developed behavior-based questions as well as by thoroughly checking references.

T$P # 77: BE PATIENT

If you are in a hurry or after a few minutes make a hasty decision that the candidate is not the right person for the job, your impatience may be evident. You have an obligation to complete an interview without giving the impression that you want it to be over. Looking at your watch or telling the candidate that you are rushed and must wrap up the interview is totally unacceptable.

To a busy manager like Heather, patience did not come easy. Always feeling overloaded, her quick 20-minute interviews that rarely started on time contributed to her bad hiring decisions. It wasn't until she made a commitment to slow down and devote her full attention to interviews that she turned her win/loss record around.

T$P # 78: DON'T OVERLOAD THE CANDIDATE WITH QUESTIONS

Take it easy. Don't make the questioning process so difficult to understand that the candidate doesn't know which question to answer first. Overloading the candidate serves no purpose and only adds to confusion. Ask your questions one at a time, and if for some reason the candidate does not understand what you said, either repeat or rephrase the question. Working from a list of prepared questions will help you avoid this problem, too.

T$P # 79: NEVER ENCOURAGE DISCLOSURE OF PERSONAL INFORMATION

Some candidates, either intentionally or unintentionally, disclose personal information during the interview. Inexperienced interviewers often believe voluntary disclosure is a license to probe into issues regarding age, marital status, national origin, number of children, etc., when in fact it is against the law to do so. The potential for allegations of discrimination becomes real. To avoid problems in this area, stick to job-related questions and don't be tempted to discuss personal issues even if the information is volunteered.

T$P # 80: DON'T DISCRIMINATE

You definitely do not want to be perceived as someone who discriminates. The best way to avoid discrimination is to stay away from questions related to a candidate's race, color, religion, sex, national origin, age, marital, or disability status. Federal laws govern these areas, and state laws may offer job seekers additional protection. Recognize your own biases and prejudices and be sure to avoid questions that are not job-related. It is your responsibility to know the laws and abide by them; the burden of proof is on you.

For example, many managers don't realize that unfair treatment on the basis of weight or physical appearance can leave them open to lawsuits. According to Cecile C. Weich, a New York City-based attorney and member of the New York Advisory Committee of the U.S. Civil Rights Commission, such discrimination is not uncommon. "We live in a society that tells us thin is beautiful," she says. Though this type of discrimination affects both men and women, Weich says women are more cognizant of discrimination than are men, and more women are seeking damages. Some businesses may not even be aware their hiring or personnel policies are discriminatory, since practices of unfair treatment are not always obvious.

Under current civil rights legislation, it is illegal to discriminate against an employee or job applicant solely on the basis of a physical or mental disability, unless it severely affects their ability to perform the job. Innocuous forms of discrimination can cost a business a significant amount of money if the accuser wins a civil suit against the company. Award amounts in discrimination cases have ranged from hundreds to even millions of dollars.

Recently approved federal policies allow your organization to be "tested" for civil rights discrimination. EEOC policy guidelines make it clear that the agency upholds the rights of any person applying for a job "whether or not a person intends to accept a position for which he or she applied." With the enactment of the Civil Rights Act of 1991, the stakes have risen, and employers can no longer afford to discriminate during hiring or at any other stage of the employment process. The best way to avoid liability is to make sure your hiring practices are nondiscriminatory.

T$P # 81: BECOME FAMILIAR WITH THE AMERICANS WITH DISABILITIES ACT (ADA)

Title I of the Americans with Disabilities Act of 1990, which took effect July 26, 1992, prohibits private employers, state and local governments, employment agencies, and labor unions from discriminating against qualified individuals with disabilities in job application procedures, hiring, firing, advancement, compensation, job training, and other terms, conditions and privileges of employment.

An individual with a disability is defined as a person who:

- Has a physical or mental impairment that substantially limits one or more major life activities;

- Has a record of such an impairment; or

- Is regarded as having such an impairment.

A qualified employee or applicant with a disability is an individual who, with or without reasonable accommodation, can perform the essential functions of the job in question.

Reasonable accommodation may include, but is not limited to:

- Making existing facilities used by employees readily accessible to and usable by persons with disabilities;

- Job restructuring, modifying work schedules, reassignment to a vacant position;

- Acquiring or modifying equipment or devices, adjusting or modifying examinations, training materials, or policies, and providing qualified readers or interpreters.

An employer is required to make an accommodation to the known disability of a qualified applicant or employee if it would not impose an "undue hardship" on the operation of the employer's business. Undue hardship is defined as an action requiring significant difficulty or expense when considered in light of factors such as an employer's size, financial resources and the nature and structure of its operation.

An employer is not required to lower quality or production standards to make an accommodation, nor is an employer obligated to provide personal use items such as glasses or hearing aids.

EEOC Cumulative ADA Charge Data
July 26, 1992–March 31, 1995
Total ADA charges: 45,053

The information provided here shows the types of disabilities that are represented in the work force along with the costs associated with charges made by disabled individuals against employers. The filing of a charge, however, does not indicate whether the charge has merit. The results show that 10 percent of the charges were related to hiring or a total of 4,806. You can substantially decrease your risk of being a recipient of a charge of discrimination by knowing which interview questions are acceptable and which are discriminatory. TIP # 82 on Etiquette for interviewing people with disabilities will be helpful.

Impairments Most Often Cited	Number	% of Total
Back Impairments	8,738	19.4
Neurological Impairments	5,354	11.9
Emotional/Psychiatric Impairments	5,243	11.6
Extremities	3,500	7.8
Heart Impairments	2,007	4.5
Diabetes	1,608	3.6
Substance Abuse	1,593	3.5
Hearing Impairments	1,360	3.0
Vision Impairments	1,257	2.8
Blood Disorders	1,178	2.6
HIV (Subcategory of Blood Disorder)	812	1.8
Cancer	1,092	2.4
Asthma	791	1.8

(**Note:** This is not a complete list; therefore, percentages do not total 100 percent and are rounded off.)

ADA Violations Most Often Cited	Number	% of Total
Discharge	22,834	50.7
Failure to Provide Reasonable Accommodation	11,819	26.2
Hiring	4,806	10.7
Harassment	4,915	10.9
Discipline	3,418	7.6
Layoff	2,272	5.0
Benefits	1,833	4.1
Promotion	1,729	3.8
Rehire	1,651	3.7
Wages	1,594	3.5
Suspension	1,015	2.3

Note: This list totals more than 100 percent because individuals can allege multiple violations; percentages are rounded off.

Note: According to EEOC, the average number of days to process an ADA charge during the first quarter of FY 95 was 297 days.

T$P # 82: PRACTICE GOOD ETIQUETTE WHEN INTERVIEWING CANDIDATES WITH DISABILITIES

It is often the social as well as the legal aspects of interviewing candidates with disabilities that are of concern to those with hiring authority. Because of this, Mainstream, Inc. provides the following basic guidelines for focusing the interview on the applicant's qualifications, as reported in *Managing Diversity* newsletter.

When interviewing *any* disabled applicant...

• Always offer to shake hands. Do not avoid eye contact, but don't stare either.

- If you feel it appropriate, offer the applicant assistance (for example, if an individual with poor grasping ability has trouble opening a door), but don't assume it will necessarily be accepted. Don't *automatically* give assistance without asking first.

- If you know in advance that an applicant has a particular disability, try to get some information before the interview on how the limitations of the disability may affect the performance of the essential functions of the job.

When interviewing an applicant who uses a wheelchair...

- Don't lean on the wheelchair.

- Make sure you get on the same eye level with the applicant during the interview.

- Don't push the wheelchair unless asked.

- Keep accessibility in mind. (Is that chair in the middle of your office a barrier to a wheelchair user? If so, move it aside.)

- Don't be embarrassed to use natural phrases such as: "Let's walk over to the plant."

When interviewing an applicant who is blind...

- Identify yourself and others who are present immediately; cue a handshake verbally or physically.

- Be descriptive in giving directions. ("The table is about five steps to your left.")

- Don't shout.

- Don't be embarrassed to use natural phrases like: "Do you see what I mean?"

- Keep doors either completely open or closed (not half opened, as this is a serious hazard).

- Don't take an applicant's cane.

- Do not touch or pet a guide dog.

- Offer assistance in travel by letting the applicant grasp your left arm, just above the elbow.

When interviewing an applicant who is deaf...

- You may need to use a physical signal to get the applicant's attention.

- If the applicant is lip reading, enunciate clearly, and place yourself where there is ample lighting.

- Communicate by using a combination of gestures, facial expressions and note passing.

- If you don't understand what the applicant is telling you, ask him or her to repeat the sentence(s). Don't pretend that you understood if that is not the case.

- If necessary, use a sign language interpreter, but be sure to always speak directly to the applicant. Don't say to the interpreter: "Tell her that..."

Reprinted with written permission of Mainstream, Inc., 3 Bethesda Metro Center, Suite 830, Bethesda, MD 20814 (301) 654-2400 (voice/ TDD).

T$P # 83: RECOGNIZE THE VALUE OF THE "POWER LUNCH"

As mentioned earlier, I don't recommend taking a candidate to lunch or dinner for the first interview. However, for a subsequent interview the restaurant setting can be very appropriate, as many candidates believe that by the time you get to the meal, the interview is over, which is actually not the case at all. You will often find that candidates will get very relaxed and incredibly honest with you concerning their likes and dislikes, strengths and weaknesses, etc. In addition, you will have the opportunity to observe table manners as I did with an executive level candidate who ate with his fingers and grunted and snorted as he wolfed down a five star meal in a New York hotel.

T$PS TO REMEMBER

1. Listen carefully for what the candidate is not saying, as it may be more revealing than what is said.

2. Don't hesitate to probe for more information if you need clarification.

3. Use the "echo" technique to probe for additional information.

4. Never be fooled by the "halo" or "horns" effect, both of which can interfere with accurate evaluation of the candidate.

5. Gather information about candidates before you invite them to question you.

6. Determine weaknesses, and you will know whether or not the candidate is the right match for the job.

7. It's important to find out if the candidate can do what is claimed. Ask candidates to explain and describe in specific detail what they claim to have accomplished.

8. Be patient, avoid stress tactics and don't overload the candidate with more than one question at a time.

9. Be aware that what you say can be seen as discriminatory. Guard against this happening by asking only appropriate questions.

10. Learn how the American with Disabilities Act (ADA) impacts interviewing.

11. Know how to interview candidates with disabilities. Good etiquette is good business.

12. Entertaining a candidate over a meal is a powerful strategy in learning more about likes and dislikes, and strengths and weaknesses.

CHAPTER 12

BRING THE INTERVIEW TO A CLOSE

Most people make a decision in the first three minutes and spend the rest of the interview backing it up. However, even if the candidate comes highly recommended or your first impressions tell you this is the one, use the interview to probe deeply. You want to get the facts to support your intuition.

—Helen Berman
Consultant

The interview should come to a close when the goals have been met. It's helpful if the hiring manager summarizes what has been discussed and determines what, if any conclusions have been reached. The candidate should be told what to expect next and not be given the feeling, "Don't call us; we'll call you."

Throughout the interview you have been presenting a positive image of yourself and your organization just as the candidates have been selling you on themselves. In actuality, everything you say and do is a portrait of you and your business. How well you come across may be revealed in the candidate's reaction to your questions. On the other hand, candidates may hold their cards close and not provide any indication of what they are thinking.

Before you conclude the interview, you will provide an opportunity for the candidate to ask questions that you must be prepared to answer.

Some individuals will have numerous, insightful questions, while others may have few or none. The number and type of questions the candidate asks will also tell you more about the individual. If questions focus on what rewards the job will bring the candidate, you may have a problem with someone who is only concerned about what they can get out of the work experience, not what they can contribute. Hiring people who are emotionally invested in the job and the organization should be your goal.

Some of the most common questions candidates ask that you should be prepared to answer are:

- What are the opportunities for growth?

- What are the short-term and long-term goals of the organization?

- What will the scope of my authority and responsibility be?

- How will my performance be evaluated and how often?

- What is it like to work for you?

- What are the major challenges of the job?

- What hours will I be working?

- When is the last time this organization had a layoff?

- Where is the person who had this job before me?

- What expansion is planned for this department, division or facility?

- How well do I meet your expectations?

- When do you plan to make a decision?

As you bring the interview to a close, you should have a good idea concerning who may be your best choice. Be aware, however, that hasty action in accepting or rejecting a candidate can be a costly mistake. Good interviewers have learned how to discipline themselves to "evaluate" candidates rather than "judge" them. There are several tips (beginning with TIP # 84) that should be considered as you wrap up the interview.

T$P # 84: SELL THE OPPORTUNITY

Only *after* you have gathered enough information about the candidate through the interview and feel as though you have identified the best candidate is it time to sell the organization and the job opportunity. Just don't oversell or make promises you can't keep. When you have answered all of the questions the candidate may have, you should be prepared to make your sales pitch. Convincing individuals that your organization will meet their career needs and allow them the opportunity to continue developing their skills has actually been taking place to some degree throughout the interview process. Sharp candidates look at every job possibility with a critical eye and evaluate each situation as they observe the interviewer and learn more about the opportunity.

T$P # 85: SHOW THE SUCCESSFUL CANDIDATE THE WORK PLACE

It's important to show the final candidate the work environment prior to making the job offer or at the very least, at the time of the offer. Neither you nor the candidate would like to be surprised. A candidate who knows that he or she will be surrounded by a 6 x 6-foot cubicle before the job is offered is unlikely to make a fuss once hired because an office with a window is not part of the package. It's also important to take the final candidate on a "tour" of the organization so that he or she can get a feel for the rest of the physical environment as well as meet future co-workers.

T$P # 86: TELL CANDIDATES WHAT HAPPENS NEXT

As the interview comes to an end, if the candidates have not already asked, feel free to let them know what will happen next. For example, if there will be a follow-up interview with another staff member, tell the candidate with whom and when the interview will take place. However, if you do not know the next step, tell the candidates you do not know but that you will get back to them. Be sure you live up to your words.

If the candidate doesn't ask, you should volunteer the next step. You could say something like:

- "I am interviewing several candidates and will be back in touch with you by the end of the week if I would like you to come back for a final interview."

  or

- "I will be making a decision by a week from today. If you haven't heard from me by Friday, feel free to call me."

  or

- "I know that I would like you to come back for another interview with one of my staff members. How does Monday at 9 A.M. sound?"

The point here is that you have an obligation to let candidates know what comes next, even if they don't ask. Everyone wants to know what happens after the final interview. Will they be asked for references? Are several finalists under consideration? Will the final decision be made within the next few days? Will those who are not selected be notified by telephone or in writing? If not selected this time, will they be considered for future opportunities? Nothing is worse than leaving candidates who have invested time in the process wondering when they will hear from you again, if ever. You owe everyone you have interviewed the basic courtesy of telling them what happens next.

T$P # 87: SAY "THANK YOU"

A simple "thank you" goes a long way in building a relationship. Whether or not the candidate is your final choice, you should sincerely thank everyone who took the time to interview. Some organizations even follow up each interview with a letter of thanks for participating in the interview. Regardless of how you do it, *it is a step that should never be overlooked.*

I consulted with a company who had a tough time attracting good candidates. They advertised, implemented an employee referral program, and even hosted a celebrity event, but still had trouble getting people to apply for their job openings. Upon reviewing step by step what they were doing during the hiring process, I discovered that they were not well organized, their managers were not educated in the fine art of interviewing, and they never said "thank you" or showed appreciation to those people who took the time to apply and interview. Upon questioning the management team, I found that they did not believe it was important to thank candidates for something the company had to offer that was a benefit to those who applied. Their thinking was distorted to some degree, but when they changed their way of handling interviews, their image in the community slowly changed, and they started to get a better response to their job openings. A simple "thank you" can go a long way in developing a positive image for you and the organization.

T$P # 88: CLOSE ON THE UPBEAT

You will have to conclude interviews with both qualified as well as unqualified candidates. With the qualified, you might wish to discuss salary and benefits at this time. Be careful not to get too enthusiastic in the event that you decide to select another individual. Unqualified candidates who are not screened out during the telephone interview and are invited to the face-to-face interview should be treated professionally. You will want to allow yourself time to make a fair judgment.

Regardless of how you feel about the candidate after completing the interview, you should end on the upbeat. You are representing your organization as a professional. If you tell the candidate that you will get back to him or her, do so in a timely manner.

T$P # 89: DOCUMENT THE INTERVIEW

Many organizations have a standard form which is used for documenting interviews. It should be reviewed prior to the interview and completed immediately afterwards. If you do not have a form, you can either purchase one or develop your own. A good resource is Business & Legal Reports (BLR), located at 39 Academy Street, Madison, CT 06443-1513: Phone Number 1–800–727–5257; FAX 203–245–2559. They provide information on what makes a good form, how to choose forms and how to design a form using the BLR book.

Many an unsuspecting hiring manager has taken notes (which were not job-related) on a resume or application. Comments about a candidate's physical appearance along with anything else that could be perceived as discriminatory should be avoided. You could be summoned to court should there ever be a charge against you, and your employment records could be subpoenaed. There is no place for comments such as "great body," "talks with a lisp," "too fat," "seems sharp for a blonde," etc. Be safe by writing notes that are strictly job-related.

A company in the South got into trouble because the hiring managers were writing comments such as those mentioned above directly on the applications for employment. I know many organizations fall prey to this inexcusable blunder, but this company was unique in that they continued to document offensive and illegal opinions even after they were sued and lost. Their philosophy has always been "we'll worry about it when it happens." It happened, but they failed to learn their lesson.

It occurred again when a candidate sued based on race discrimination because of comments that were made on the application, which the candidate saw when the interviewer allowed an interruption and left the room for a few minutes. It was an enormous battle, and the company lost again. It was no slap on the wrist this time. Their negligence almost cost them the business. Don't ever think something like this can't happen to you. There are EEOC charges and suits of this nature filed every year throughout this country.

T$PS TO REMEMBER

1. It's important to sell your organization to the candidate, but only at the end of the interview.

2. The final candidate should see where he or she will be working so that there are no surprises later.

3. Every candidate, whether final or someone in the first interview, should be told what the next step will be.

4. Always close with a "thank you" and in a friendly and positive manner even if you do not plan to hire the candidate. Leave a good impression on everyone.

5. Document the interview but never write anything on the resume or application that could be taken as discriminatory.

PART 4

REFERENCES

Not without it's hassles, checking references takes time and effort and is a task that some managers would rather skip. Yet a survey conducted by Globe Research Corp. for *Recruitment Today* magazine indicates that 96 percent of all of their respondents conduct background checks, primarily for employment verification (98 percent) and for job performance information from a former employer (91 percent). Almost two-thirds of the randomly selected survey participants verify degrees, licenses and other credentials. An employer has the right to ask about a candidate's prior employment and to follow up with written or verbal inquires to the previous employers. The problem is that many companies, concerned with lawsuits, have adopted a policy that only verifies the former employee's dates of employment, position and salary. This is prudent on the previous employer's part, but not very helpful to the person checking the references.

Concern about the high cost of losing suits or even successfully defending them has made many employers afraid to say anything. Individuals have even collected damages by claiming that a former employer's silence forced them to defame themselves. One employer had to pay $200,000 for giving the following reference: "The employee was fired for failure to increase business as a major-product sales representative." In other cases, awards have exceeded $3 million dollars. It seems to make sense that a sure way to avoid lawsuits is not to reveal any information about former employees and that is the challenge facing many hiring managers who want to check references. No one wants to talk, or so it seems.

"Say too much, and risk a lawsuit; ask too little, and risk a lawsuit." As frustrated as you may feel, chances are that your own organization has a similar policy concerning the release of information to prospective employers. This practice has become so pervasive that several attorneys, who were quoted by the Bureau of National Affairs in its *Daily Labor Report*, said it is nearly impossible for companies to get adequate references on job candidates.

Unfortunately by making it more difficult to get references, these same policies are contributing to another problem. There are "negligent hiring" lawsuits that involve employers who hired people who became violent on the job. If employers are asked to give references and withhold negative information about an employee's violent past, the employer could conceivably be held liable if the worker later injures someone.

One example involved a security guard who worked at a bank in Miami and shortly after starting his new job, killed another guard. Attorneys for the victim's widow found that the employee had a history of strange behavior and sued the bank for negligently hiring the murderer and for failing to adequately check prior employment references. The bank settled the lawsuit with a payment of $300,000.

In another case in Colorado, a three-year-old boy was sexually assaulted by a McDonald's employee while on the job. The child's family sued alleging that a complete reference check had not been completed and that if it had, the check would have revealed that the man had a history of sexually assaulting children. The family sued, and a jury awarded them $210,000.

So what can a hiring manager do to get the information needed concerning education, salary and accomplishments? Don't give up. Remain aggressive and involve the candidates by asking them to provide the documentation and information you need. If they want the job bad enough, they will find a way. What kind of success are employers having in checking references when honest references are difficult to get and candidates are suing former employers who give them bad references and are winning? More success then most people believe possible. The tips in Part 4 will help you get what you need to make a good hiring decision as well as stay within the law.

If you feel you must solicit opinions or your organization requires that you do so, the hiring manager should always be the one to actually speak with the references. Here are some ideas that will make checking references easier:

- Ask to speak to the person who directly supervised the candidate. State the reason for your call (to help in identifying and verifying employment information related to the job for which the candidate is being considered).

- Assure the reference that everything discussed will remain confidential.

- Ask questions from a prepared list that are related to the specific job and skills needed to perform the job.

- Document each answer you ask and the response. Quote the exact words of the reference if possible or at least paraphrase.

CHAPTER 13

GET REFERENCES TO OPEN UP

Hiring the right people is a vital function that could determine the success or failure of a business. It's no secret that good employees mean profit, and bad hiring decisions create nothing but problems that stay with you for a long time. It takes a definition of job requirements along with good interviewing skills and reference checks to recognize high performance team players when you see them.

—Marci Zied
Owner, Uniglobe Travel Agency

How much information you gather has a lot to do with your skill in communicating with references. Since it's impractical to check references in person, the most efficient way to speak with references is by telephone. Using a telephone reference check form as a guide for each call will force you to stay organized and help you ask the same questions about each of your final candidates. Keep in mind, however, that there are two types of references. The first is for verification of facts that include dates of employment, job titles, salary, and education. The second part of the process is soliciting information that may or may not be factual. Unless you personally know the reference with whom you are speaking, you have no way of truly knowing whether or not what is said is an honest description of the candidate. For example, often when people are fired, someone feels sorry for them and if that someone is a reference, he or she may make highly favorable comments that are not accurate. On the other hand, some candidates get bad references that are totally unjustified from former supervisors who hold a grudge. Half-truths are another problem that are difficult to detect. All references should be considered as only one part of the hiring process. The interview is still the best way to determine suitability for the job.

You will be talking to former supervisors and human resource professionals, the latter of whom will be the least helpful in most cases, because of their strict adherence to company policy regarding providing reference information. Start with immediate supervisors; if the candidates have done their job, the supervisors will be expecting your phone call. As you get started, it's imperative that you build rapport so that references feel comfortable enough with you to be honest.

Three simple steps will help you build rapport with references:

- Identify yourself, your organization and reason for calling. If the reference hesitates, offer your telephone number and suggest that he or she call you back (collect, if necessary) to verify your identity.

- Verify the information provided by the candidate, such as dates of employment, job title and responsibilities, reason for leaving, and salary. Ease into questions by asking closed questions that can be answered by a "yes" or "no" before moving onto more challenging questions.

- As soon as you feel that the reference is willing to volunteer additional information, shift from closed to open questions.

A sample conversation might sound like this:

You: "Good morning. My name is Carol Hacker. I'm the Accounting Manager for XYZ company. John Doe has given me your name as one of his references. Is this a convenient time to spend a few minutes talking?"

Reference: "Yes, this is fine. How can I help you?"

You: "I'd like to begin by verifying some information. Mr. Doe indicated on his resume that he worked for you from October, 1982 until the present. Is this correct?"

Reference: Yes, he was an Accounting Supervisor when he first started in 1982 and moved up to his most recent position as Controller in 1990."

You: "He also shared with me that he supervised up to as many as eleven people over that time. Is this correct?"

Reference: "Yes, he initially had two direct reports, but as his responsibility increased, the department grew and when he left, he had eleven people reporting to him plus several part-time personnel who helped out during our busy season."

You: "Mr. Doe said he was earning a base salary of $48,000 plus bonus. Is this right?"

Reference: "I believe so. I hesitate because I'm not exactly sure on the figure, but you could verify that number with the Human Resources Department. It sounds about right."

You: "You can understand how important it is for us to find the right individual for the job, not only for our benefit, but also because I wouldn't want to hire someone who wouldn't be happy here or didn't work out and I had to let him go. The new job should be a 'win-win' for both sides. With that in mind, I'd like to ask you some additional questions about Mr. Doe."

Reference: "Fine."

You: "Supervisors don't necessarily manage each of their employees the same. Some people are easier to manage than others. What kinds of people did John Doe find difficult to manage and why?"

Reference: "That's a tough question. John is a good manager. If he found an employee challenging or difficult to manage, it would be someone who did not pay enough attention to detail. Let me give you an example. Since payroll administration was in John's area, he was, of course, always concerned about accuracy. He inherited a payroll clerk who made lots of mistakes. He worked with her, but eventually they both agreed she was not suited for the tedious work required. Rather than terminate her, he found another job for her within the company where she, I might add, has excelled."

You: "Can you give me an example of a time when John lost his temper with one of his employees, which we all know can happen to any of us if we are pushed far enough?"

Reference: "Yes, there is a time that comes to mind..."

As you can see by this hypothetical example, I eased into the conversation with the reference by building rapport and starting with some easy questions. I gradually moved toward more difficult questions as I felt that the reference was feeling more comfortable with me. I continued to ask questions from my prepared list until I was satisfied that I had a good picture of the candidate from the reference's perspective.

Remember, the telephone reference check is an interview and requires a high degree of professionalism. The key to getting references to be honest with you is convincing them that the information they could potentially provide is critical in order to make an objective hiring decision. You want to give the candidate fair consideration, but you can only do that if you know strengths as well as weaknesses as identified by you during the interview and shared by the reference in person or by telephone.

Your best chances for getting the information you need may hinge on your level of confidence, persistence and assertiveness. The reference must also know that anything said will remain strictly confidential. I know of several instances where candidates were allowed access to their personnel files after they were hired and saw what their references said about them. It was not a good situation.

T$P # 90: RELEASE EMPLOYERS FROM LIABILITY

To protect yourself and your organization, consider having an attorney draw up an authorization form that candidates can sign to release former employers from any liability associated with providing references. Or list the information you need and ask the candidate to sign a separate release indicating that he or she understands that former supervisors will be contacted. Former employers are more likely to give references if they know the candidate has agreed. Some organizations include on the Application for Employment form a statement that references will be checked. Candidates will be asked to sign the form releasing the employer from any liability.

T$P # 91: DECIDE ON THE BEST WAY TO COMMUNICATE WITH REFERENCES

Many of us take for granted the fact that we can pick up the telephone and call the references as listed. However, a personal, face-to-face reference check, is still the best way to get the information you need. Employers are likely to be more candid with you in person. It may not be practical to arrange a meeting, but worth the extra effort especially for senior level candidates.

The least effective method of gathering information about candidates is by writing to previous employers. Some organizations ask candidates to sign a release form and send the signed document to the candidate's references with expectations that they will be completed and returned. Many employers don't have the time or the interest in preparing written references. Don't hold your breath in waiting for written references to arrive.

The telephone is the best method of choice for most employers for two main reasons:

• You can get the information you need immediately.

• It's a relatively inexpensive way to gather information and verify what you already know about the candidate as well as probe for additional facts.

Through your discussion, you may get information that will lead you to check further regarding some part of the candidate's background, qualifications, education, etc., and that follow up can also be done efficiently by telephone.

T$P # 92: MAKE THE MOST OUT OF CONTACTS

The telephone reference check is an indisputable vital link in the selection process; it's not enough to rely on the word of the candidate. You will be contacting "strangers" and asking for their time to talk about their former employees. Plan your questions in advance and include specific questions that will help clarify anything about which you are concerned. Respect the time of those who are willing to talk to you and stay focused in your conversation.

T$P # 93: BE PREPARED TO HANDLE RESISTANCE

There are several things that you can do to break down the barriers between you and the reference. Often reluctant to share information for good reason, references are still worth contacting, as many will give in and tell you what you need to know. A friend of mine who is a human resource manager does a great job in getting references to open up. He is always friendly and quickly engages people in non-threatening dialogue. He gradually moves toward the questions he has prepared and often gets much more information than he asked for. He even got to know one reference so well that they decided to meet for a round of golf. It can be done if you take a few minutes to plan your approach.

The following steps are a guide for getting information from references who are reluctant to talk:

- Encourage references to be candid with you by being friendly. A positive approach toward anyone who is tempted to be resistant can make a difference. Talk with a smile in your voice and quickly get to the point of your call.

- If possible, try to find out in advance something about the person you're about to contact for a reference. You may find something in common, the same hobby, interest in sports, etc. One way to get this helpful information is to ask candidates during the interview to tell you something interesting about their supervisor.

- Say something good about the candidate. Former employers who have agreed to be references are often pleased to hear that people who once worked for them, and in some cases people they personally chose to hire, are recognized as competent by others also.

- Keep your questions neutral so that you don't offend or lead the reference. For example, you might say something like: "How does the candidate handle pressure or can you give me an example of a time when the candidate was under a lot of pressure?" Avoid questions like: "Can you tell me about a time when the individual flew off the handle or blew up when criticized?" Your choice of words is the key here. Don't say anything that would put the reference on the defensive.

T$P # 94: KNOW WHAT TO ASK

As you develop your questions in advance, think about your job requirements. You will want to ask questions that help you gather the information you need to verify facts, as well as confirm your own opinions concerning the candidates. You may not ask any questions that would be illegal if they were asked of the candidate. You may also not require a candidate to provide the name of a member of the clergy as a reference. A reference of this type could be viewed by the EEOC as a way of determining the candidate's religion. All questions should be job-related, and there must be consistency in the things you ask of references for each candidate. Ask different people different questions, and you lose your ability to compare candidates.

If you are checking references on managerial candidates, you will want to explore the candidate's management style, leadership experience and ability, and specific strengths and weaknesses as they relate to the position for which applied. You will also want to find out how comfortable the individual is with delegating, disciplining and organizing. Your goal is to hire the candidate who will provide the greatest long-term investment for your money.

The following sample questions should be used only as a guide. If you have any doubt as to whether or not the questions should be asked, seek professional advice:

• The candidate said that the reason for terminating employment with your organization was... Is this correct? If this is not correct, please explain.

• In what capacity did this person work for you?

• How would you evaluate the candidate's overall work performance?

- This is what the candidate would be doing for our organization. How do you think his or her skills and abilities would fit into the position?

- When there was something that needed immediate attention, what did the candidate do to address the situation?

- What are the candidate's greatest strengths?

- In what areas are additional improvements needed?

- I'd like to read you a description from his or her current resume. (Stop at each significant accomplishment and ask for comment).

- If you had the opportunity to rehire this person, would you?

- How did the candidate happen to be hired by your organization?

- Is there anything else I should know about the candidate's work performance?

- What reservations, if any, should I have about hiring the candidate?

In checking references for non-managerial candidates, your focus will be slightly different. You will still need a list of quality questions but because of the nature of the jobs that fall into this category, your approach will be slightly different. You will ask questions that cover day-to-day performance including how well the candidate gets along with managers. You will also want to find out how closely the candidate needs to be supervised. Can the individual work well with little direction or must someone be there at all times to oversee?

Some of the questions you may want to use are as follows:

- Give me two examples of things the candidate has accomplished that demonstrate willingness to take directions.

- Tell me about a time when the candidate was criticized. What was the reaction?

- How would you describe the candidate as an employee?

- What can you count on this person for without fail?

- Tell me about the candidate's ability to take on responsibility.

- What does he or she need to do to continue to grow professionally?

- What has been the most difficult part for you in managing the candidate?

- How does the candidate compare to the other employees who work for you?

- Tell me about a time when he or she had a disagreement with you.

- How well does the candidate get along with peers?

- Give me an example of a time when the candidate had a confrontation with someone else in the department.

- How would you rate his or her quality and quantity of work?

Whether checking references on a management or non-management candidate, you need to get a good idea of how the candidate will fit into your organization and the best way to do that is by preparing for this step in the hiring process.

T$P # 95: VERIFY EDUCATIONAL REFERENCES

Checking educational references is important because it's a known fact that many candidates not only falsify resume information concerning work history, but also lie about education. In some cases, it is the name of the school from which they claim to have graduated. In other instances, it's the fact that they never got a degree at all, much less in the discipline indicated. Some lie about scholastic achievement or simply don't volunteer the fact that their 4.0 average was on a 5.0 scale, not a 4.0

scale as you had thought. This creative license to manipulate the data often goes unnoticed by inexperienced hiring managers. Protect your organization by checking educational references, too. Ninety-seven percent of colleges and universities will verify attendance and degrees for employers. These records provide helpful data that's easy to obtain.

Many employers have found the perfect match only to discover that the candidate did not tell the truth on the resume or application. A case in point left a very unhappy candidate not only without an offer but no job on the other end as he prematurely gave notice to his employer that he was leaving the company. Little did he know that the potential employer thoroughly checked references and found that he had not completed college as he had indicated on his resume. The job offer was rescinded. The company started looking again, and the candidate tried to argue for his old job back.

When verifying educational credentials, you will want to ask questions concerning the following:

- Dates attended.

- Major and minor areas of study.

- Courses taken that are relevant to the position for which the candidate is being considered.

- Degree(s) earned.

- Honors received.

- Attendance record (this may be difficult to get as many colleges and universities do not track attendance, but most high schools do).

- Internships and work-study programs in which the candidate participated.

- Grade point average including breakdown for major area of study.

T$P # 96: SEEK-OUT REFERENCES

Hiring managers are often discouraged because they believe that references will not talk to them but only verify "factual information." This is not necessarily so, especially when you consider the fact that there are other alternatives. Besides, most candidates will give you only their best references, which makes it hard for you to get a true picture of the candidate from an outsider's perspective. The best references are those who directly supervised the candidate. Ask for two or three supervisors, a peer and someone else who is familiar with the candidate's work. Network if you have to find people with the candidate's previous employers who may be useful. Just be sure you speak with a cross-section of references so as to balance any differences of opinion.

If the candidate is still employed, you will most likely need references other than people at the company for which the candidate works anyway. Some alternatives are:

- Co-workers.

- Subordinates.

- Previous supervisors.

- Customers.

- Vendors, suppliers.

- Consultant who has worked with the candidate.

- Members of professional associations to which the candidate belongs.

- Former professor or teacher (if recent graduate).

- Business people in the community.

If the candidate cannot come up with references, you should be concerned. Put the responsibility on the candidate to find people with whom you can talk. If they can't come up with solid references, you may decide not to give the candidate further consideration.

I remember a very impressive candidate for an entry-level customer service position. She had all of the right answers and had impeccable credentials. When it came time to check her references, she had none. She claimed that two of her three last employers had gone bankrupt and that the last one, which was her current employer did not know she was looking for another job, and she did not want anyone contacting them. I explained to her that it was our company policy that we had to speak with a minimum of three work-related references. She held her ground, and I did not hire her. I later found out that she had been fired from her previous two jobs for stealing money from the petty cash box. Checking references is worth the time and effort.

T$PS TO REMEMBER

1. Have candidates sign a release from liability form so that references will feel more comfortable in giving information.

2. Use the telephone to check all but senior-level positions (ideally done face-to-face but usually not practical).

3. Chances are you may encounter resistance from those who are not willing to provide you with useful information. Be prepared to handle their reluctance.

4. Have a list of questions that you can ask. Keep in mind that you should ask the same questions for those being considered for the same position. You may not ask anything during the reference check that you could not legally ask of the candidate in person. This includes questions related to race, sex, religion, national origin, etc.

5. Don't overlook the importance of checking educational credentials. Many applicants falsify information to appear more qualified.

6. Personal references have little or no value and should be avoided.

7. If you can't get the information you need, look for others who may know the candidate and could tell you something about his or her work performance.

CHAPTER 14

LIMIT YOUR LIABILITY

Convince former supervisors to disclose information about a candidate's past performance by placing them in the role of evaluator and advisor on the person's future abilities.

—Paul Falcone
Manager of Staffing & Development
Aames Financial Corporation

Aside from limiting your liability, checking references can also reduce turnover. A February, 1995 article in *HR Magazine* referred to an article by J. Douglas Phillips ("The Price Tag on Turnover") published by *Personnel Journal* in 1990. The Phillips article was based on a case study by the Rutgers University Graduate School of Management, which demonstrated that turnover costs averaged about 1.5 times the annual salary of the position in question. Thus, an employee earning $30,000 a year would cost his or her employer $75,000 ($45,000 + $30,000) if he or she left the company after twelve months. He goes on to say that most of the costs associated with turnover are "hidden expenses and account for 80 percent or more of turnover costs." Most of these hidden expenses come in the form of lost productivity.

It's apparent that checking references can prevent a bad hiring decision and the resulting costs of turnover. However, what some people who check references fail to recognize is that references are not necessarily a true reflection of what the candidate can do. Checking previous employment references can be a difficult task as well as a sensitive issue. The sensitivity comes in because of well-publicized damages awarded to employees by former employers who said or publicized dishonest or libelous information. However, verifying facts is important but often not considered as important as the answers to other questions we ask. The danger lies in relying too much on references that are not factual. Unless you personally know the references and truly understand their value system, you are primarily seeking opinions and judgments. If you feel you must solicit opinions or your organization requires that you do so, the hiring manager should always be the one to actually speak with the references.

Here are some ideas that will make checking references easier:

- Ask to speak to the person who directly supervised the candidate. Identify yourself by name, title and company. State the reason for your call (to help in identifying and verifying employment information related to the job for which the candidate is being considered).

- Ask questions from a prepared list that are related to the specific job and skills needed to perform the job.

- Document each response. Quote the exact words of the reference if possible or at least paraphrase.

In conducting a retained search, I reached the point of having to check references and spoke with four references for each of the final candidates. One of the three final candidates had references which provided conflicting information about him. One confirmed that the candidate had been a supervisor while two of the references could not recall him ever having supervised anyone. I immediately became suspect. I even called the candidate thinking I had misunderstood what was said. In reality, he had been a supervisor but the references he chose had not been prepared for my phone call and had confused him with someone else. Any time you discover an inconsistency, find out through further questioning what really took place or what is actually correct.

T$P # 97: CHECK REFERENCES ON FINALISTS ONLY

It's a waste of time and money to check references of candidates who are not finalist or serious contenders for the job. Some employers make the mistake of checking references after the first round of interviews, before the finalists have been identified. I know several organizations who have even checked references before meeting the candidates. In these cases references were listed on the resume. It was a total waste of time.

T$P # 98: DON'T DELEGATE THE TASK

Something as important as checking references should ideally be done by the hiring manager, for it's this person who best understands the job requirements and what type of person would be most suited for the job. However, if you find you must get someone to help, be sure the individual knows what you expect and can effectively communicate with references.

Some businesses hire companies to check references for them. I have not been particularly impressed with those companies I have worked with because I felt they never truly understood the needs of the organization and in some cases did little more than a superficial check, which was almost worthless. If you decide to use an outside firm to handle this important part of the hiring process, make sure you feel totally comfortable with what they plan to do and the questions that will be asked. Find out which company does a good job in this area and check references on them before asking for their help.

I am aware of an organization who always delegated this responsibility to the receptionist of the company as they felt she had plenty of "free time" in between telephone calls. The problem in taking this approach was apparent. She was not educated in the finer points of how to conduct a thorough reference check, didn't know the candidates about whom she was talking, and often was interrupted by calls coming into her switchboard and had to put the reference on hold several times during the conversation.

T$P # 99: DON'T ASK FOR PERSONAL REFERENCES

Asking the candidate for personal references is a waste of time. Neighbors, doctors or lawyers can provide little useful information regarding the candidate. You need to speak with people for whom the candidate has worked. At the very least, speak to a co-worker who can offer some perspective on how the candidate interacts with other members of the team. I know that some organizations still ask for personal references and some employment applications require personal references, but that doesn't mean those references have any value.

T$P # 100: TAKE WRITTEN LETTERS OF REFERENCE WITH A GRAIN OF SALT

Some candidates will present a written reference or two along with their resume or application or even hand them to you at the end of the first interview. Many letters of reference are written at the time of termination. No one in their right mind would write something negative and hand it to a just released employee unless it was anything but positive or at the very least neutral. I never put too much confidence in a written letter of reference. What I may do, however, is call the individuals who signed the letters and consider them a bona fide contact. I then ask them the same questions I ask each of the other references.

T$P # 101: FOLLOW UP ON INCONSISTENCIES

As you speak with references, you may come across inconsistent information. Hypothetically, the candidate may have indicated on the application form that she supervised 33 people in her last job. That can be verified. If the information given does not check out with the reference, probe for more information. You may also find inconsistencies in opinions concerning the candidate. If this happens, dig deeper for additional details and clarification.

T$P # 102: CONDUCT CREDIT CHECKS CAREFULLY

It's acceptable and advisable to conduct a credit check if the position requires that the employee is involved with company finances or highly sensitive issues. Credit checks are regulated by the Federal Fair Credit Reporting Act (FCRA) as well as state laws. The employment application must notify the applicant that an investigation may be made to obtain information about the individual. The purpose of the notice is to help protect the company from a subsequent suit by an applicant for invasion of privacy or defamation. However, the applicant's agreement to the background check is no guarantee against a lawsuit but does mitigate the level of risk. The purpose of a credit check is to protect the organization against loss and theft and also against actions brought by others if the employee acts on your behalf.

The Federal Fair Credit Report Act provides applicants and employees with the right to know what's in their credit file. If you deny employment to an applicant based upon a credit report, the applicant must be told it is the reason for rejection. You must also give applicants the name and address of the consumer reporting agency so that they can get a copy of the report and correct errors if necessary.

Investigations concerning the financial status of applicants such as a credit check tend to have an adverse impact upon minority groups and single women and may be viewed as a violation of EEOC laws if challenged. You will want to proceed with caution if you decide that checking credit history is important.

T$P # 103: DOCUMENT

Make clear notes that you can review later when comparing candidates. Just like the interview, it's difficult to keep information from getting confusing if you are speaking with three or four references for each of your final candidates. A simple form can help you stay organized.

One hiring manager struggled with the whole documentation process and finally decided that all she needed to do was slow down the conversation so she could make adequate notes. She also developed a simple form that had some multiple choice questions that could quickly be circled and also included some open questions to which the answers would be helpful when making a final decision. These two techniques made her job of checking references much easier and a responsibility she no longer dreaded.

The following sample reference check form could be used or you can create one of your own:

Sample Reference Check Form

Name of Applicant	Name of Reference
Position Applied For	Company
Location/Department	Telephone Number

Verify:

1. Dates of employment from _____ to _____
2. Job Title _____
3. Job Duties _____
4. Salary data _____
5. Reason for leaving _____

Here are some sample questions you may use:

1. In what capacity did this person work for you?

    _____
    _____
    _____

2. How would you evaluate the candidate's overall work performance?

    _____
    _____
    _____

3. This is what the candidate would be doing for our organization. How do you think his/her skills and abilities would fit into the position?

    _____
    _____
    _____

4. When there was something that needed immediate attention, what did the
    candidate do to address the situation?

    _____

    _____

    _____

5. What are the candidate's greatest strengths?

    _____

    _____

    _____

6. In what areas are additional improvements needed?

    _____

    _____

    _____

7. I'd like to read you a description from his current resume. (Stop at each
    significant accomplishment and ask for comment).

    _____

    _____

    _____

8. If you had the opportunity to re-hire this person, would you?

    _____

    _____

    _____

9. How did the candidate happen to be hired by your organization?

    _____

    _____

    _____

10. Is there anything else I should know about the candidate's work performance?

    _____

    _____

    _____

11. What reservations, if any, should I have about hiring the candidate?

    _____

    _____

    _____

Completed by_____Date_____

T$P # 104: EVALUATE WHAT YOU HEARD

Only you can decide whether or not what you heard is what you need to know in order to make an informed decision. It's sometimes hard to remain objective; we like some people more than others. The old gut feeling may enter the picture again and that's OK as long as you recognize the fact that relying solely on intuition for your decision can be costly.

Some hiring managers check references but really only go through the motions. They decide who they want based on who they like best and not necessarily who is the most qualified. They hear only what they want to hear and when it comes down to evaluating each of the finalists, it is no contest. Use a form to evaluate references to help stay focused and on track.

T$PS TO REMEMBER

1. Don't waste your time checking references unless the candidate is a serious contender for the job.

2. Always check the references yourself. Don't ask someone else to perform this very important task.

3. Skip personal references, as they have little or no value.

4. If candidates give you written letters of reference, remember that no one would write anything less than neutral in a letter of this type. To get a complete picture of the candidate, contact the author of the letter by telephone.

5. Anything that is inconsistent should be discussed further until you are satisfied with the answer.

6. If you feel there is a business necessity to make a credit check, be sure you let those candidates who are rejected because of a bad credit rating know why. There may be an explanation that they have the right to share.

7. Document your findings in order to avoid confusion later.

8. Evaluate what you heard before making the final decision. You might want to use an evaluation form to help you compare candidates and ulimately select the one who is most suited for the job.

PART 5

MAKING THE FINAL
DECISION

Research supports the idea that the last person interviewed is three times more likely to be hired than the first person interviewed. With that information, it may or may not be apparent that many people who are responsible for hiring decisions do not have a system. Without a method for comparing candidates against one another, it is easy to make the wrong choice.

The astounding costs associated with turnover that are directly related to bad hiring decisions are broken down and re-printed with written permission of WGL's Human Resources Policies and Practices Services (1994, Warren, Gorham and Lamont) as a final reminder that the costs of bad hiring decisions are both obvious and hidden but, nonetheless, have a major impact on employers of all sizes.

Separation Costs:

- performance documentation

- performance improvement plan development

- performance plan review

- severance pay

- exit interview (cost of interviewer's and employee's time)

- COBRA benefits continuation costs

- unemployment compensation payments

- social security payments

- administrative record keeping

Replacement Costs

Recruitment

- job evaluation
- job description
- advertising
- campus visits and recruiting
- minority and other targeted recruiting programs
- employment agency or search firm fees
- temporary agency fees
- employee referral program
- recruiting materials
- resume screening time
- resume tracking
- administration or record keeping
- correspondence and communication

Selection

- initial screening interviews
- application/resume tracking and review
- reference checks
- credit and security checks
- interviewing time for human resources department
- interviewing time for managers

- pre-employment skill testing

- pre-employment drug testing

- pre-employment medical examinations

- referral program payments

- travel costs

- tours

- correspondence and communication

Training Costs

Orientation

- site tours

- human resources department staff time

- managerial time

- co-worker time

- orientation materials

- administration or record keeping

Training

- planning and design of programs

- training materials

- trainers (internal and external)

- time of the managers

- time of the co-workers

- educational courses

- on-the-job training

- salary and benefits (until employee picks up speed)

Productivity Costs

- substandard production

- reduced production

- down production time

- quality control costs

- increased costs in waste

- increased error rate

- overtime

- temporary staff replacement

- idle production

- unfilled orders

- morale of employees assuming the extra workload

- stimulation of additional turnover

- loss of supervision and management to hiring and training tasks

- work team disruption

- increased workload

- increased job insecurity

- corporation reputation

- increased injuries

The tips in PART 5 offer guidance as you come down the home stretch toward a final decision. As a hiring manager you started the selection process by defining your job requirements; you carefully screened applicants and entered into a relationship during the interview. You've checked references and now you have the responsibility for the final decision. How you assess the final candidates is the last step, which only the hiring manager and those who interviewed the candidate can take.

CHAPTER 15

"DON'TS" TO CONSIDER BEFORE YOU DECIDE

> Every hiring decision has an impact on an organization's financial health. Decisions rest on the ability to predict behavior and judge character. In an effort to combat the costs associated with a bad choice, managers everywhere should be educated and held responsible for their actions.
>
> *Training Magazine*

You've probed for clues to behavior and explored work experience. You've gathered information and listened rather than volunteered information prematurely. You've sold the organization, and you are now ready to compare candidates. Or are you? No doubt by now you know more than you ever wanted to know about the impact of your hiring decisions. Morale and productivity, along with other hidden costs, have hopefully alerted you to what follows a bad decision.

In the *Gold Collar Worker* by Robert E. Kelley, the author describes turnover as a "contemporary plague" and estimates turnover on average to be 30 percent annually. Often a result of bad hiring decisions, turnover is a major problem. An employer with 1000 employees can expect up to 300 people to leave in a year's time! No wonder the costs of doing business are climbing yearly. Will you avoid a bad hiring decision every time? Unfortunately, no, but you have already greatly improved your odds for making the right choice the first time just by reading this book. As the selection process comes to a close, there are some "don'ts" that should be considered before making a commitment.

Ellen was a highly respected manager in a bank. She had a reputation for attracting talented professionals and successfully beating her competition in hiring the best of the best. One day Ellen made a mistake that lead to a series of problems including an EEOC decision which was not in her favor. The action was ruled in violation of Title VII. The bank was charged with race discrimination in hiring. There were no written job descriptions or clearly defined criteria for hiring, which was very unlike Ellen. Against her better judgment, she hired someone based solely on potential and physical appearance. Although attractiveness and neatness were accepted as selection criteria based on business necessity, she still lost the case. Some said she was "conned" by a pro who made a living "testing the waters" of discrimination. Whatever the situation truly was, the bank had defense fees along with damages to the plaintiff to pay. Perhaps, if she had thought about the "don'ts" more carefully, she would have done differently.

As you get ready for the final phase of the selection process, take into account some of the things you don't want to do, beginning with TIP # 105.

T$P # 105: DON'T BE CONNED BY A PRO

If you encounter candidates who seem too good to be true, they probably are. Slick and prepared for all of your tough questions, dressed impeccably, giving all of the "right" answers could mean you have met someone who is out to charm you into believing you can't live without them. Candidates today are being coached and coddled by experts who know how to convince you that they are the best choice. Can you blame them? It's no fun being without a job, especially when you've been employed all of your adult life and suddenly find yourself unemployed. Desperate and eager to get your offer, polished candidates may not always be the "pros" you'd hoped for.

Although there are no guarantees, there are several steps you can take to prepare yourself so that you are not conned by a pro:

• **Interview thoroughly.**

Do your homework. Plan for the interview and develop or select questions that will get the candidate talking. Then listen carefully to each response.

- **Probe anything with which you feel uncomfortable.**

The interview is your chance to clarify anything that's on the resume or application. It's also the time to ask for explanations if you're not sure what the candidate means or you are uncomfortable about something that's said.

- **Check references until you are satisfied with what you've heard.**

This is often overlooked by inexperienced interviewers. Not only should you check references, but you should keep pushing until you have enough information. If you are not satisfied with the caliber of references, or the references are reluctant to share information, go back to the candidate and tell him or her you need some help.

- **Ask other staff members to interview the candidate.**

Getting others involved, as long as they understand the importance of their role in interviewing and are qualified to do so, is recommended. Input from other members of your team can provide invaluable insight that you may have overlooked.

- **Don't allow the candidate's personality to overshadow his or her weaknesses; don't hire someone based upon their appearance either.**

Your decision should not be based primarily on gut feelings, but rather on whether or not you are convinced that the candidate can meet your expectations and do the job as defined. Many hiring managers have been conned by a pro. Unfortunately, once you've made a bad hiring decision, the costs start mounting up quickly. From the intangible costs to the hard dollars associated with turnover, once you've discovered your mistake, impact on the overall efficiency and worker morale can lead to undeniable problems. If there's any doubt in your mind about whether or not to hire someone you think may be deceptive, clear up any questions before you extend a job offer.

T$P # 106: DON'T HIRE THE FIRST PERSON INTERVIEWED

I've seen hiring managers get so excited about the first candidate they interviewed that they cancelled the rest of the interviews and hired the first person with whom they spoke. You owe it to yourself to select the most qualified individual. If you've done a good job of screening, you should interview all of the candidates you planned to interview. You may think the first candidate is the best possible choice, but you won't know for sure until you interview the others.

A business owner seeking a top level executive to run a division of his company used a search firm to help him locate and then narrow down the field of candidates. The final four candidates were to spend a full day each with him. After the end of the first day, the owner called the search firm to tell them he had no interest in interviewing the other three top candidates. When questioned, he said he was so impressed with the first candidate that he knew the others could not begin to compare. The firm convinced him that he needed to follow through with his commitment to interview the others not only for their sake, but for his own.

He reluctantly agreed to proceed with his original plan and when the end of day four came, he had completely changed his mind. The fourth candidate was by far the best fit for the job. The owner was elated with his final choice. If he had offered the job to the first person interviewed, he would never have known what he was missing. The end result was an excellent choice that almost didn't happen.

T$P # 107: DON'T BE AN "IMPULSE BUYER"

Like Christmas shoppers on December 24, some managers wait until the last minute to fill a vacancy and end up hiring whomever comes along. One manager put it this way: "Managers absolutely must avoid the pitfalls of being impulse buyers and last minute shoppers."

One way to avoid this problem is to keep a resume file of potential candidates that can be referred to whenever there is a position to be filled.

Another method is to plan ahead for the unexpected by reminding yourself that you could have a vacancy at any time for a variety of reasons.

Jim, an officer of a large family-owned business, fits the profile of the impulse buyer. He always seems to wait until the eleventh hour to hire someone, which often means a costly mistake. One day a manager in the company had a heart attack on the job. She was a key employee and was responsible for over 200 people. Jim was frantic with worry about who would fill in for her or maybe even take her place. After three months off of work, the employee retired on disability, and Jim knew he had to find a replacement. He had one of her best employees filling in for her, but he wasn't satisfied with the results.

Unfortunately, Jim had not kept a resume file, but filled his waste basket with hundreds of unsolicited resumes he received every month. He called several agencies, but he knew that would take time. He placed an ad in the local newspaper that brought about 50 responses. He interviewed and selected the first person he "liked" without fully considering the job requirements of the position. He was totally unprepared for the loss of an important supervisor. When push came to shove, he fell into his old habit of "buying" on the spur of the moment, which was disastrous.

T$P # 108: DON'T HIRE A GENERAL WHEN YOU NEED A SERGEANT

If a candidate is overqualified for a position but is willing to accept your offer because he or she desperately needs a job, or just wants to get a foot into the door of your organization, chances are the individual will never be happy. Such candidates may even be a thorn in your side for the rest of their tenure with you. Don't make a hasty decision if you are unsure about the match. Use the interview as the vehicle for weeding out people who are not the right fit. Generals are committed to leading others and seldom will be happy and productive as followers.

Many managers make this mistake as did Ted, who hired a young woman who had her heart set on not what she was hired to do as a secretary, but what she wanted to do, and that was become a manager. Ted always looked for opportunities to promote from within and immediately recognized that the woman had a lot of talent. Unfortunately, he didn't recognize the fact that she had no intention of being a "Sergeant" but expected to move up almost immediately and become a "General." That of course was impossible, and the new employee soon quit.

If you explain expectations to final candidates and conduct a thorough interview that includes questions about goals and future aspirations, you run less of a risk of selecting people who do not want to do the work for which they are hired.

T$P # 109: DON'T SELECT SOMEONE BASED SOLELY ON POTENTIAL

Inexperienced hiring managers sometimes get excited about a candidate, forget about the job requirements they've established and hire someone based on their "potential" for success. It's fine to know that a candidate has potential to learn and progress, but using potential as the primary reason for hiring someone can equal a bad hiring decision.

A major corporation did exactly this when they started hiring candidates because of potential. They didn't even have job openings, in some cases, in which to place the newly hired individuals. It continued as managers built empires of personnel who had a lot to offer but were just not qualified for the openings available. Employees sat around and played cards and read books when times were slow. Finally the company had a major layoff. Four thousand people lost their jobs. The company was overstaffed, and people who were hired and told, "don't worry, we'll find a place for you," were soon standing in unemployment lines.

T$P # 110: DON'T REJECT CANDIDATES IMMEDIATELY

Hasty decisions made without getting to know the candidate are not only unfair to the candidate, but to yourself as well. Looking back on past interviews, how often have you rejected candidates without giving them a chance? Bad hiring decisions are often associated with rejecting candidates before you get to know them.

Many times we know after the first interview that the candidate is not the right match. Telling a candidate immediately after the interview that you have no interest or that the candidate is not what you are looking for is only asking for trouble, especially if you detect a poor attitude or negative personality. It can lead to arguments, a potential charge of employment discrimination or even physical violence. You are better off to notify all candidates in writing of your decision after everyone has been interviewed and the final candidate selected.

T$P # 111: DON'T LET THE PRESSURE GET TO YOU

The responsibility of hiring the right person for the job can be overwhelming. If your organization doesn't have a human resources department and the job of screening, interviewing and hiring falls in your lap, it can mean a lot of pressure. The trick is to learn how not to let it get to you, and that can be difficult.

If you need someone and you need them now, you may feel the pressure to make a quick hiring decision, one you could regret for a long time. Don't let yourself succumb to the urge to rush the process. Some organizations skip the telephone interview, others do a poor job of developing questions, while some take a short cut by not checking references. Don't cheat yourself by giving into time constraints. Get in the habit of planning ahead whenever possible so you're not pressed for time.

T$P # 112: DON'T MAKE THE OFFER UNTIL ALL SCREENING AND TESTING IS COMPLETE

If part of your screening process requires that the candidate submit to a physical exam, drug test, pre-employment test or other screening device, be sure the activity is completed, and that you have the results before you extend a job offer. Because of time constraints and an eager-ness to hire someone immediately, some organizations actually put people on the payroll before the results of the tests have come back. In some cases, when it becomes known that the candidate did not pass one or all of the tests, the individual who is already officially an employee is terminated. You can avoid this trap by waiting until results are in before making someone an employee.

A company who required a pre-employment drug test was so pressed to hire people to fill vacancies that they did not wait for the test results to come back before officially hiring them. When test results indicated drug use, they found themselves in the uncomfortable position of having to terminate employment and tell an angry new employee why. Fortunately, this organization no longer follows this practice on the advice of their attorney.

T$P # 113: DON'T MAKE A JOB OFFER WITHOUT A MUTUAL UNDERSTANDING OF SALARY, BENEFITS AND EXPECTATIONS

Every candidate should have enough time to ask and have answered any questions concerning salary, benefits and expectations by the end of the final interview at the latest. In fact, all three of these areas should be defined in writing before the search begins and discussed with final candidates prior to the offer. Later, the expectations can be incorporated into the performance appraisal.

Some of the benefits which you should be prepared to discuss are as follows:

personal days

extra vacation

medical insurance

dental insurance

life insurance

short-term disability insurance

long-term disability insurance

deferred compensation

stock options

company paid pension

immediate vesting of pension accrual

matching investment

profit sharing plans

annual physical

legal, tax, financial assistance

loans

discount on purchases of company product

tuitional reimbursement

executive development

professional association memberships

subscriptions

expense accounts

company car

gas allowance

relocation allowance or benefit

relocation assistance for spouses

These are not all-inclusive but will give you an idea of the types of benefits that organizations have to offer. Every organization doesn't offer every benefit, but identifying those that apply to you will help you prepare for a discussion of benefits with the candidate.

T$P # 114: DON'T BE INFLUENCED BY "BEAUTYISM"

Although we all should know that beauty is only skin deep, there seems to be a temptation to hire people who are attractive, sometimes regardless of their lack of skill or failure to meet job requirements. It is considered discriminatory not to hire people whom you judge to be "unattractive" even though they meet your job requirements.

For example, an attractive receptionist may be a pleasant thought but without the necessary qualifications, you are running the risk of being viewed as discriminatory in the selection process, not to mention the fact that you have just increased your chances of making a bad hiring decision.

T$P # 115: DON'T HIRE IN YOUR OWN LIKENESS

Managers who skip the steps in the hiring process and feel they know exactly what they are looking for sometimes fall into the trap of hiring someone just like themselves. There are pros and cons to hiring a team of people who are very similar in personality. However, diversity is wonderful, and with it comes creativity and different ways of solving problems and leading an organization. Before you hire another person who is very much like you, think about the down side to such a decision.

It was a joke among employees at a large beverage company, that employees not only were alike in personality, but that they all looked similar. The men were generally under 5'10" with dark hair and eyes. The women were 5'2" weighing 100–110 lbs. with blonde hair and blue eyes. Some call it cloning; however you want to describe it, hiring in your own likeness can be a real let down and rob the organization of the talent it needs to succeed.

T$P # 116: DON'T HAVE TOO MANY FINALISTS

Hiring managers sometimes fail to narrow down the field of candidates perhaps because they don't have a clear picture of what it is they are looking for. In any event, too many finalists can confuse the decision. Set a goal to limit your finalists to no more than five–three would be better. If you've done a good job of interviewing, you should be able to identify the top candidates without a problem.

T$P # 117: DON'T HAVE TOO MANY DECISION MAKERS

Although several people may have been involved in the interviewing process, it's important to limit the number of people who will make the final decision. The more people involved, the longer it takes. In addition, the manager to whom the new employee will report should have the final say.

A large company in the transportation industry implemented a team approach to hiring. However, decisions became very complicated when numerous decision makers were asked for input on the final choice. The company eventually abandoned their approach and went back to a more traditional method of decision making. More is not always better.

T$P # 118: DON'T SETTLE FOR SECOND BEST

I once made the mistake of settling for second best and learned a lesson I will never forget. I had been hired into a position as Human Resource Manager and desperately needed an assistant. I had been working 10 to 12 hour days, sometimes 7 days per week for 9 months, and I was exhausted. I struggled to find the time to begin the search process; it was a vicious circle, but I knew I had to start somewhere. My husband and I had scheduled a trip, and I was determined to go. I was open to working with an employment agency and of course, they were appreciative of the business. To make a long story short, I accepted what I knew was not exactly what I needed and wanted in a new employee. We took our vacation. When I returned to work, I knew I had made a big mistake and ended up paying dearly for the decision to settle for second best.

T$P # 119: DON'T BE OFFENDED BY POST-OFFER QUERIES OR COUNTER-OFFERS

A manager, who was not accustomed to interviewing and felt uncomfortable with counter-offers in response to a job offer, was not only offended when a candidate tried to negotiate the offer, but actually threatened to withdraw the job altogether. His immaturity almost cost him a very qualified new employee. The candidate actually saved the day by convincing him that it was very common for job seekers to negotiate or counter an offer.

Some candidates may have lots of questions. Some may even counter your job offer for more money and/or benefits. Don't be caught off guard should this happen. Making a counter offer is an accepted and sometimes even an expected practice. You may or may not be in a position to offer more. If you feel uncomfortable negotiating a job offer, there are a several good books on negotiating that include information on how to handle job offers and counter-offers.

T$P # 120: DON'T ASSUME THAT CANDIDATES WILL WAIT INDEFINITELY

If you believe that qualified candidates will hang around and wait for an offer forsaking all other offers until they hear from you, you're wrong. Disappointed hiring mangers are kicking themselves as we speak for dragging their feet in making a decision. Top performers always seem to be in short supply. Some employers take months to make a decision. If you are serious about someone, don't waste time. Check references and make a decision. Good candidates are often lost due to unnecessary delays.

T$PS TO REMEMBER

1. Any candidate who appears too good to be true should be a sign that you should conduct an especially thorough interview and reference check before making the final decision.

2. Resist the temptation to make a quick decision and hire the first person you interview.

3. Never make hiring decisions on impulse because you don't have a talent bank and need someone immediately.

4. Hiring a General when you need someone who will fulfill the basic job duties of a Sergeant can be a costly hiring mistake.

5. Potential is important, but don't hire someone solely on what he or she may someday be able to accomplish. You need someone who can perform the job as defined now.

6. Never hire until the results of all pre-employment tests have been reported to you.

7. Limit your finalists as well as your decision makers.

8. Expect post-offer queries and counter-offers and be prepared for them.

9. Make a job offer as soon as you know you're ready in order to avoid losing a good candidate who is expecting or hoping to hear from you.

10. Compensation is not, and never has been, the number one motivating factor for candidates in accepting job offers.

CHAPTER 16

"DO'S" OF THE JOB OFFER

Sometimes it's obvious that none of the available candidates could fill the bill. That's where foresight comes into the picture. It should have been used a long time ago to foresee and avoid such a predicament.
—from *Bits & Pieces*

Of all of the decisions that businesses make, bad hiring decisions are the costliest because they inevitably lead to economic woes. As you prepare to make a job offer, you will want to be ready for negotiations. Senior level candidates are most likely to engage in aggressive counter-offers. You may even have entry-level candidates ask for more money or perks in exchange for compensation. It is an expected practice in the hiring process, so don't be surprised if a candidate flinches at your offer and enters into negotiations with you.

Several things you will want to be prepared for when you make an offer include the following:

- Decide what you are willing and not willing to negotiate prior to extending the job offer.

- Review salary expectations. If during the first interview or telephone screen you asked the candidate about salary history or requirements, you already know what the candidate expects to be paid.

201

- Consider offering perks in lieu of money, especially if you can't quite meet the salary expectations. Extra goodies such as tuition reimbursement, company paid dues for association membership and compensatory time off will help to sweeten the pot.

- For executive level and some management positions, you may want to consider offering an employment contract as an incentive either at the time the individual joins the organization or later as an additional reason to accept your offer now.

- If you can't meet salary expectations at the time of your initial offer, you may want to consider a "sign-on" bonus of a flat amount in order to entice the candidate.

- If the candidate is relocating and you had not planned to pay relocation costs, this is an area in which you may want to make a concession. Offering mortgage assistance or paying the real estate commission on the sale of the candidate's house, whether in part or in full, could be the deciding factor.

- You may find yourself in a situation where the candidate's current employer makes a counter-offer in a last attempt to get your final choice to change his or her mind. It's difficult for you to influence the candidate's thinking at this point, and you will want to mentally prepare for this possibility.

As you read the final chapter in this book, you will find some additional tips for making the process of extending a job offer more comfortable.

Also, remember that employees are looking for the following rewards, according to a Gallup Organization pole, and if they don't find what they are looking for, money will not necessarily be an incentive:

1.	Good health insurance	81%
2.	Interesting work	78%
3.	Job security	78%
4.	Opportunity to learn new skills/training	68%

5.	Paid vacation	68%
6.	Ability to work independently	64%
7.	Recognition from peers	62%
8.	Regular hours	58%
9.	Opportunity to help others	58%
10.	Low job stress	58%
11.	**High income**	**56%**
12.	Proximity to home	55%
13.	Chances for promotion	53%
14.	People contact	52%
15.	Flexible hours	49%

T$P # 121: DO GIVE THE TOP CANDIDATE ENOUGH TIME TO EVALUATE THE OFFER

It's unfair to ask a candidate to make a decision regarding your offer on the spot. Depending upon the position, it is reasonable to allow the candidate several days to two weeks to give you an answer. You have invested a lot of time and energy to this point; don't blow it by putting pressure on the top candidate to make a hasty decision and potentially be a problem for you. What you are willing to accept from an unskilled worker versus a candidate for vice president obviously varies greatly. Just be alert to the fact that unreasonable expectations can lead to the potential loss of your first choice.

T$P # 122: DO CONFIRM THE JOB OFFER IN WRITING

You will want to prepare a written job offer after the candidate accepts your verbal offer. It's the best way to ensure that there are no misunderstandings concerning salary and benefits. You don't have to be a large organization in order to extend your offer in writing; it should be done regardless of your size.

Your letter should include:

* A welcome and congratulatory statement.

* Job title.

* Start date.

* Pay/salary rate.

* Contingencies such as the candidate must pass a company physical, complete a satisfactory background check and submit documents to verify date of birth, proof of citizenship, etc.

A sample letter follows:

Date

Mr. John Doe
Street address
City, State, Zip Code

Dear John:

We are pleased to confirm your acceptance of our offer of employment for the position of Customer Service Manager, reporting to Jane Smith, Vice President of Sales, at a starting salary of $0,000 per month.

You will be eligible to participate in our comprehensive benefits program, which includes a health plan for you and your eligible dependents. The current coverages and protections afforded by this program will be discussed with you during orientation.

The Immigration Reform and Control Act of 1986 requires employers to have documentation verifying new employees hired as of November 6, 1986 to be either a U.S. citizen or alien legally in the country and authorized to perform work. You are required to complete the I-9 form as part of the Immigration regulations. You must provide the original (copies will be made upon review) of the following on or before your effective date of employment to verify legal status:

a. U.S. passport, Certificate of U.S. Citizenship, Certificate of Naturalization, unexpired foreign passport if endorsed by the Attorney General, or green card with photo or other identifier approved by the Attorney General regulation.

or,

b.   A social security card or birth certificate and a driver's license or other state identifier with photo.

You will also be required to satisfy company standards with regard to background and reference checks, and also company medical standards. Such standards will include, but will not be limited to, a screening for the presence of illegal and/or controlled substances in your system. Satisfying the company medical standards, which includes passing a drug screen, is a condition of employment. Failure to satisfy the medical standards, a positive screen for drugs, or refusal to take the drug screen will constitute grounds for withdrawal of the company's employment offer. Once we have received the results of the background and reference checks and the medical evaluation, we will be able to confirm your employment date.

We look forward to working with you. Welcome to XYZ Corporation.

Sincerely,

Sue Brown
Manager

T$P # 123: DO KEEP IN TOUCH

After you have extended an offer and finalized a start date, make an effort to stay in touch. Send updated information about the company and call to say you are looking forward to the day he or she starts. Don't take the relationship for granted; you've come too far. Often there is gap of several weeks or more between when the job offer is extended and the individual starts work. You increase the risk if you don't maintain contact of losing the individual to another job offer or a change of heart.

T$P # 124: DO FOLLOW UP WITH UNWANTED CANDIDATES

Rejecting candidates you don't want to hire is uncomfortable for most people. However, it's important that you follow up and offer the common courtesy of at least telling them that another candidate was selected. You don't have to go into detail as to why you made another choice; just don't leave someone who has invested their time with you wondering what happened.

A sample letter of regret follows:

Date

Ms. Jane Doe
Street Address
City, State, Zip Code

Dear Jane:

Thank you for your interest in XYZ Corporation. We have interviewed a number of highly qualified people and have selected another candidate for the position. Your resume (or application) will be kept on file for one year. Should another opening come up for which you are qualified, you will be considered.

Thank you again for taking the time to meet with us. Best wishes for your continued success.

Sincerely,

John Smith
Accounting Manager

T$P # 125: DO BE PREPARED FOR A "NO THANK YOU"

There is no guarantee that the candidate you want the most wants to work for you. Perhaps money is an issue because you cannot meet the candidate's salary expectations. What do you do next? You can offer the job to the next most qualified individual or start your search over again. To convince candidates who don't seem interested in the job that they should reconsider is not a good idea. People who have already made up their mind will be a poor risk in the long run.

If your first choice turns you down and your second and third choice are not a match, you may have a problem. It's expensive to go back to the drawing board and start the hiring process all over again.

There is, however, something you can do as you take another look at your alternatives:

- Review your job requirements and circle the three most important.

- List skills that can be easily learned in a short period of time.

- Identify training that could be implemented to help cut the learning curve.

- Take another look at your second and third choices and consider their ability and willingness to learn.

- Decide whether or not one of the choices would be acceptable with some extra help.

- Offer the job to your second choice if you feel confident in your decision.

A company was extremely disappointed when their first choice refused their offer. Initially, they thought that no one else they had interviewed could handle the job. Upon further consideration, they changed their minds and hired their second choice after considering what it would take to get additional training for the individual. During the orientation, the hiring manager even told the new employee that she was not his first choice. He wanted her to hear it from him before she heard it from someone else. She appreciated his sensitivity and worked hard to learn the job. Today she is one of the superstars in the company. She was a great choice after all.

T$P # 126: DO CONSIDER A NON-COMPETE AGREEMENT

You may want to have new employees sign a non-compete agreement if they have access or contact with highly confidential information. In the agreement employees agree that while employed with the company, and for a specified period thereafter, they will not engage in any activities that compete for business against the enterprise. Some states have laws that govern non-compete agreements. Others, for example, prohibit them unless they are executed when the employee is first hired or immediately after a promotion. Some states allow non-compete agreements with certain restrictions.

T$P # 127: DO USE A SYSTEM FOR COMPARING

In the final rating of candidates, you may want to select or develop a form for rating candidates against your job requirements. It's often difficult to choose between several very qualified people.

References will help confirm your preliminary thoughts, but there are several other factors that you may wish to take into account which may help determine the winner:

- Review job requirements and the job description again to think about each of the finalists in relationship to each.

- Take another look at the candidate's work history and relevant education.

- Evaluate each candidate's response to questions in terms of verbal answers, as well as body language.

- Consider the candidate's salary expectations in conjunction with what you can afford to pay.

- Look at each candidate's potential to learn and eventually be promoted.

Only by assessing each candidate's qualifications will you be able to determine whether or not you have got the right person for the job. This is the time to consider gut feelings or intuition, perhaps, as a deciding factor.

The following sample Interview Rating Summary Form and instructions for using it may be helpful as you evaluate each candidate:

Instructions for Using the Sample
Interview Rating Summary Form

1. Complete *Applicant Name, Interviewer Name, Date of Interview, Date Applicant is Available for Work, Position Applied for.*

2. List additional *Critical Job Requirements* (those requirements that you want to evaluate during the interview) in addition to *relevant education, work experience, communications skills and interpersonal skills,* which are already listed for you.

3. Assign each *Critical Job Requirement* an *Importance Factor:* 1 (least important); 2 (somewhat important); and 3 (very important). Write that number in the far left-hand box that corresponds with each *Critical Job Requirement. Each importance factor may be used more than once.*

4. After the first interview with each applicant, indicate under the column *Job Requirements* whether the applicant (2) exceeds; (1) fully meets or (0) does not meet the *Job Requirements.* **It is <u>imperative</u> that if you decide to select this method of rating applicants, that you justify your reason for your scores in writing on the lines provided under each *Critical Job Requirement.***

5. To score: Multiply your *Importance Factor* by the number you have rated for *Job Requirement.* Place the score in the box marked "score" on the right side of the form.

6. Sub-total at the bottom of the first page by adding down the numbers in the "score" column on the right of the form.

7. Enter the Sub-total from page 1 onto the second page in the box provided.

8. To Total: Calculate total score by adding down the numbers in the "score" column on the right side of the form (including the sub-total). Write the number in the box marked "TOTAL."

9. All applicants being interviewed for the same position must be evaluated against the same *Critical Job Requirements.*

SAMPLE INTERVIEW RATING SUMMARY FORM

Applicant Name _____ **Date Available** _____

Interviewer _____ **Position** _____

Date of Interview _____

Importance Factors
3=most important
2=next most
1=least important

Critical Job Requirements

Job Requirements
2=exceeds
1=fully meets
0=does not meet

To Score:
Multiply
Across

_____	RELEVANT EDUCATION	_____ _____
_____	WORK EXPERIENCE	_____ _____
_____	COMMUNICATIONS SKILLS	_____ _____
_____	INTERPERERSONAL SKILLS	_____ _____
_____		_____ _____
_____		_____ _____

Page 1 of 2

Sub-total Score by Adding Down

SAMPLE INTERVIEW RATING SUMMARY FORM

Applicant Name _____ **Date Available** _____

Interviewer _____ **Position** _____

Date of Interview _____

Importance Factors 3=most important 2=next most 1=least important	**Critical Job Requirements cont.**	**Job Requirements** 2=exceeds 1=fully meets 0=does not meet	**To Score:** **Multiply** **Across**
_____	_____	_____	_____
	_____		
	_____		
_____	_____	_____	_____
	_____		
	_____		
_____	_____	_____	_____
	_____		
	_____		
_____	_____	_____	_____
	_____		
	_____		
_____	_____	_____	_____
	_____		
	_____		
_____	_____	_____	_____
	_____		
	_____		
		Sub-total from Page 1	
	Page 2 of 2	**TOTAL Score by Adding Down**	

T$P # 128: DO PREPARE FOR ORIENTATION

It's easy to ask someone to join your organization, but what do you do on the first day? All of the work that has gone into the hiring process could be lost if you do a poor job of helping the new employee get off on the right foot. Whether you have a formal orientation or a simple explanation of what happens within your organization, you need to be absolutely sure your new employee feels welcome and understands expectations. It may sound like a logical statement, but many new people are lost because they don't feel like they belong. They have left behind their support system and everything familiar to them to join you.

Some organizations use mentors with all new employees to be sure new people have someone to turn to in learning the subtle ropes. New employees should also be introduced to the job in stages. A job description should be given to the individual and instructions and training should be part of the orientation. It's also appropriate to take the new employee on a tour of the facility, especially if you did not do so as part of the final interview.

A new employee also needs to know the organization's policies and procedures. Many employers have an employee handbook that should be reviewed with the individual, in addition to holding regular meetings with the employee to answer questions and assure understanding of expectations. If you have a probationary period, you may have benchmarks by which you measure the employee. It's important that you meet regularly to discuss progress. It's a costly decision if you decide to let the employee go.

The following sample orientation checklist form can be used to assure that all employees get the same basic orientation information and can be adapted to meet your specific needs:

SAMPLE NEW EMPLOYEE
ORIENTATION CHECKLIST

Employee's name_____Date_____

Job Title:_____

Welcome

( ) Tour the department, plant or company

( ) Introduce employee to other employees

( ) Explain the functions of each person as you introduce them

( ) Show where restrooms, breakroom area and parking facility are located

( ) Explain organizational structure

Policies and benefits

( ) Time sheet

( ) Payroll procedures

( ) Insurance information

( ) Salary reviews

( ) Performance reviews

( ) Vacations

( ) Holidays

( ) Leaves of Absence

( ) Sick leave

( ) Expense reports

General information

( ) Employee handbook

( ) Bulletin boards/Company newsletter

( ) Keys

( ) Security card

( ) Lunch and breaks

( ) Area restaurants

( ) Telephone system

( ) Office equipment

( ) Supplies

( ) Housekeeping

( ) Mail procedures

( ) Credit cards

Introduce the new employee to the job

( ) Ensure working area, equipment, tools, and supplies are ready

( ) Explain levels of supervision within the department

( ) Schedule training

( ) Order business cards (if appropriate)

( ) Provide job description

T$PS TO REMEMBER

1. Allow time for the candidate to whom you have offered the job enough time to evaluate your offer.

2. Always confirm the offer in writing so there is no misunderstanding later.

3. If the candidate is not scheduled to start work immediately, stay in touch to reduce the risk of a change of heart.

4. Always call or write to candidates who did not get the job as a basic courtesy.

5. Expect that there will be times when candidates reject your offer. Don't take it personally. Decide whether or not your second choice is an acceptable alternative.

6. Non-compete agreements are used by many businesses and may be something you want to consider.

7. Find a way to compare finalists and measure skills and experience against your job requirements.

8. Never be unprepared for the new employee. Even a basic orientation is better than nothing.

APPENDIX A

QUESTIONS

The following questions are a guide and are not meant to be all-inclusive. As you choose questions that you may want to ask during the job interview, start by deciding what questions are appropriate for the position you want to fill. Consider developing questions of your own based upon your job requirements. Later, determine at what point during the interview you want to ask the questions you've selected. Some are better asked during the first or telephone interview, while others should be left for the final meeting with the candidate.

The most important thing to remember is that all of your questions should be job-related. If you have any doubt about what you can and cannot ask, don't ask. The questions provided here are offered with the understanding that neither the author nor the publisher is engaged in the business of rendering legal service. If legal advice is required, the services of a competent attorney should be sought.

Education

1. What did you like best about school? Least?

2. What are you most proud of achieving during your school years?

3. Did you do your best in school? If not, why not?

4. What did you spend most of your time doing in school?

5. What course did you enjoy the most?

6. What course did you find the most valuable?

7. What course did you find the least valuable?

8. Describe your most rewarding high school/college experience.

9. What was your major? How did you choose it?

10. If you had it to do over again, would you have chosen the same course of study? Why or Why not?

11. Are your grades a good indicator of what you learned?

12. Which school year was the most difficult? Why?

13. If you could change something about your school years, what would it be?

14. Have you ever cheated or been tempted to cheat on a test? Tell me about it.

15. If you had it to do over, what would you do differently in school?

16. Did you ever fail a class? If yes, what was the reason?

17. What was your rank in your graduating class in high school? College?

18. What would your instructors say about you?

19. Were your favorite teachers easy or demanding?

20. Tell me about a time when you had a difficult time getting along with a teacher.

21. Have you ever tutored another student? If so, what did you gain from that experience?

22. What courses did you take that are directly transferable to this job?

23. What extracurricular activities did you participate in?

24. Give me an example of something you learned that you can apply to your work as a result of participating in extracurricular activities.

25. What activities did you enjoy the most?

26. What extracurricular activity did you not participate in that you wish you had?

27. How did you select the college you attended?

28. How has high school/college prepared you for the "real world?"

29. What makes you unique as a result of your educational experiences?

30. What are your plans for further education?

Work Experience

1. Describe your activities during a typical day on your last or current job.

2. What were your major responsibilities?

3. What were some of the toughest parts of that job?

4. Who did you report to and who reported to you?

5. What responsibilities/tasks took most of your time?

6. Describe the most significant project you have worked on so far?

7. Have you held other positions like the one you are applying for? Tell me about them.

8. How much time did you spend working alone in your last or present job?

9. How much travel was required?

10. What did you like most about your last or most recent job?

11. What special skills and knowledge did you need to perform your duties in your previous jobs?

12. Give me two examples of things you've done in previous jobs that demonstrate your willingness to work hard.

13. How have you benefited from your work with your last company?

14. What could your past employers count on you for without fail?

15. In what ways have your previous jobs prepared you to take on greater responsibilities?

16. What kind of career progress did you make in your last job?

17. What was the most disappointing aspect of your last job?

18. In your last job, what problems did you identify that had previously been overlooked?

19. How do you feel about how your last organization was managed?

20. Tell me about the most boring job you ever had.

21. Describe a time when you encountered obstacles in your last job while you were in pursuit of a goal. What happened?

22. How did you feel about your workload in your last job?

23. What did you do in your last job that made you more effective?

24. In your last three jobs, what were your job titles and how important were those titles to you?

25. Do you think you were fairly compensated for the work you did? Why or why not?

26. If you were to hire someone to replace you in your last job, what kind of person would that be?

27. What would you expect of your replacement during the first thirty days on the job?

28. What suggestions did you make in your last job to increase profits, improve morale, cut costs, increase output?

29. How many hours per week did you find it necessary to work to get the job done?

30. How long have you been out of work?

Initiative/Motivation

1. Which of your ideas and actions helped you move up in your present/prior organization?

2. How do you start a project when you get no direction from your supervisor?

3. What risks did you take in your last or present job? Tell me about it.

4. When is it OK to break the rules?

5. Tell me about a project that you were responsible for initiating.

6. What would you like to have done more of in your last job? What held you back?

7. In your last job, how was your approach to the work different than in jobs you held before?

8. What did you do to make your last job more interesting?

9. What three things have you done on your last job that have given you the most satisfaction? Why?

10. Tell me about your efforts to "sell" a new idea to your boss.

11. How do you reward and encourage others?

12. Tell me about a suggestion you made on the job to improve the way things worked. What was the result?

13. Have you ever felt as if you had outgrown a job? Tell me about it.

14. Tell me about a time when you reached out for additional responsibility.

15. What have you done in your last job that makes you feel proud?

16. What kinds of rewards are most satisfying to you?

17. How do rewards like bonuses affect your work performance?

18. What motivates you to put forth your best effort?

19. Can you give me an example of how you have been creative?

20. Why do you think initiative is important?

21. Tell me about a time when you used competition as a means of encouraging others do their best.

22. In what areas do you feel you would like to develop further? How will you do that?

23. What aspirations do you expect to satisfy by accepting this position?

24. How did you handle your biggest career disappointment?

25. In your opinion, what does it take to be a "success?"

26. Give me an example of a time when you recognized others in order to encourage them.

27. What does it take to challenge you?

28. Tell me about a project you really got excited about.

29. What have you done that shows initiative?

30. What have you done about your own professional development in the last five years?

Leadership/Management

1. How would the people who work for you describe you?

2. Tell me about a time when you conformed to a policy with which you disagreed.

3. What motivates you to lead others?

4. How do you measure your success as a leader?

5. Describe your leadership style.

6. What personal characteristics are necessary for success as a leader?

7. What kinds of problems does your staff bring to you?

8. Tell me about a time when you had to be especially tactful in handling a problem.

9. What makes you an effective leader?

10. What leadership skills do you have that might account for your success thus far?

11. Tell me about a time when you had to lower your standards.

12. What single skill or ability is your greatest asset? How did you develop this expertise?

13. How have you used your position as a leader to get what you want?

14. Give me an example of a time when you were put on the spot.

15. What would it be like working for you?

16. What do you think could potentially interfere with your effectiveness as a leader?

17. Tell me about a time when you had to challenge someone else's way of thinking.

18. Describe the relationship you feel should exist between the manager or supervisor and those reporting to him or her.

19. What does being a leader mean to you?

20. Give an example of a time when you had to be assertive in order to get your point across and still not offend.

21. In what kind of environment are you most comfortable?

22. What kind of hours do you typically work?

23. What kind of experience have you had in strategic planning?

24. Describe a project you were responsible for that required a high amount of energy over a long period of time.

25. Tell me about a time when you were asked to complete a difficult assignment even though the odds were against you. What did you learn from that experience?

26. What do you do to assure that you have enough time to follow through on set objectives?

27. In each of your last three jobs, what were your most tangible contributions?

28. What aspects of your job do you consider most crucial?

29. What do you enjoy most about being a leader? Least?

30. Tell me about a time when someone at work complemented you on your management skills.

Interpersonal Skills

1. What kinds of people do you get along with the best?

2. What kinds of people irritate you?

3. How would you describe yourself as a communicator?

4. Describe a time when you came up with a creative solution to a problem between two employees.

5. Define "good communication."

6. Tell me about the toughest proposal you've ever written.

7. What have you done to improve your verbal communication skills?

8. On a scale of 1 to 10, how well do you think you listen?

9. On a scale of 1 to 10, how well do you think your employees would say you listen?

10. What are you doing to improve your listening skills?

11. How do you handle employees with an attitude problem?

12. How do you communicate with a shy or nervous job candidate during the interview?

13. How important is communication on your present job?

14. What kinds of things do you enjoy teaching others to do?

15. How does your boss get your best out of you?

16. What do you do to encourage others to do their best?

17. For what advice or assistance do your co-workers turn to you?

18. Tell me about a time when you had to handle a highly emotional employee.

19. How would you handle an employee who changed from a reliable, hard working employee to a problem employee?

20. How do you persuade others to your way of thinking?

21. What would you do if you found yourself working for someone who could not control his or her temper?

22. Tell me about a time when you caused a breakdown in communication at work.

23. What would you do if a co-worker was depressed and talked of suicide?

24. Tell me about a recent success you had with an especially difficult employee.

25. Tell me about a time when your boss criticized your work.

26. How do you assert yourself in order to get what you need?

27. What would you say to an employee who is frequently late for work?

28. How would you discuss your job dissatisfaction with your boss?

29. What do you do when an employee comes to you with a personal problem?

30. Tell me about a time when someone at work complemented you on your management skills.

Sales

1. Jobs have pros and cons. What do you see are the pros and cons of selling?

2. What can you contribute to our sales team?

3. What qualifications do you have that make you a successful sales person?

4. How many accounts do you prefer to handle at one time?

5. In what kind of work environment are you most comfortable?

6. If I hired you, what kind of training do you think would be needed to improve your skills?

7. How motivated are you by money?

8. Tell me about the most important account on which you have ever worked.

9. How does this position fit in with your long-term career goals?

10. We have all failed to meet a quota at one time or another. When you don't meet your goals, how do you handle it?

11. What was the sales volume in your territory when you took over? What was it when you left?

12. Tell me about the most difficult sale you ever made.

13. How would your customers describe you?

14. What kinds of customers upset you?

15. What support do you feel would be necessary from the company for you to open a new territory?

16. How much job-related travel is too much?

17. What do you get from selling that you couldn't get from any other work?

18. How do you handle rejection?

19. Which type of selling gives you greater satisfaction, frequent small successes or many turndowns followed by a big success?

20. How do you stack up against your competition?

21. Why can you sell for us in a way that no one else can?

22. What do you know about our product line?

23. How would you go about selling our products and/or services?

24. What kinds of products and/or services have you sold in the past?

25. What is involved in selling your products and/or services?

26. What benefits do you stress when selling your current products and/or services?

27. What are the 3 keys to successful telephone sales?

28. Tell me about a marketing campaign you developed.

29. Tell me about a time when you turned an occasional buyer into a regular buyer.

30. By what percentage have you increased the sales volume in your territory?

Problem Solving/Decision Making

1. What steps do you take to solve a problem?

2. How do you enlist the help of others in solving a problem?

3. What do you want your staff to do when they encounter problems?

4. Tell me about a time when you eliminated or avoided a problem before it happened?

5. What unconventional methods have you used to solve problems?

6. What criteria do you use to make decisions?

7. How long does it typically take you to make a decision?

8. What is the last decision you made before leaving your present or last organization?

9. What kinds of decisions are the most difficult for you to make?

10. We all make errors in judgment from time to time; tell me about the last time you made a judgment error.

11. Describe the way you handled a major problem in your last job.

12. Once you've solved a problem, what do you do to follow up?

13. What kinds of problems are you best at solving?

14. Give an example of a problem you solved which required documentation.

15. What is the worst decision you have made in a previous job? Why did you make it? How did you correct the problem?

16. What analytical tools do you use in solving problems?

17. If a co-worker needed help in solving a problem, but you did not have the time to help, what would you suggest?

18. What was your greatest success in solving a difficult problem?

19. To whom did you turn for help the last time you had a major problem?

20. How do you evaluate alternative solutions to problems?

21. Tell me about a time when many people were counting on you and you failed to solve the problem.

22. How do you go about identifying a problem?

23. How do you keep from jumping to conclusions when attempting to solve a problem?

24. Tell me about a recurring problem that you would have liked to solve in your current or last job but haven't yet.

25. To what extent has your last job required you to be a good problem-solver?

26. What types of decisions did you make on your last job?

27. Tell me about a time when you had a limited amount of time to make a difficult decision.

28. Tell me about a time when you had to make an unpopular decision.

29. What do you do when priorities change quickly? Give me one example when this happened.

30. Tell me about a decision you made while under a lot of pressure.

APPENDIX B

PRE-EMPLOYMENT INQUIRIES

Most managers know that there are certain questions that should not be asked during the interview, as they are in violation of Equal Opportunity Employment laws and regulations. However, it's not always obvious which questions are acceptable and which are discriminatory. The following questions provide an overview but are not intended to be all-inclusive. In addition, there are individual state laws that govern what employers may and may not ask during an interview, which of course would vary according to where the interview takes place. Laws change. If you have any doubt about what you may or may not ask, seek legal counsel.

It's also important to note that if a candidate volunteers information such as age, number of children, religion, etc., you should not ask for details; you must discourage the candidate from talking further. And under no circumstance should you write down what is being said as it could be used against you later if the candidate does not get the job. The most appropriate step to take, should a candidate volunteer information of this nature, is to redirect the conversation toward job-related issues only.

SUBJECT: **NAME**
Acceptable: "What is your full name?"
                 "Have you ever used an alias? If so, what was the name you used?"

	"What is the name of your parent or guardian?" (Ask only if the applicant is a minor.)
Discriminatory:	"What is your maiden name?" (Permissible only for checking prior employment or education.)
	"Have you ever changed your name by court order or other means?"

SUBJECT: **RESIDENCE**

Acceptable: "What is your address?"

"What is your telephone number?"

Discriminatory: "Do you rent or own your home?"

"Who resides with you?"

"How long have you lived in this country?"

SUBJECT: **AGE**

Acceptable: "Do you meet the minimum age requirement for work in this state?"

Statement that being hired is subject to verification that applicant meets legal age requirements.

"If hired, can you show proof of age?"

"Are you over 18 years of age?"

"If under eighteen, after employment, can you submit a work permit?"

Discriminatory: "Where were you born?"

"Where were your parents, spouse, and/or other relatives born?"

"Are you a U.S. citizen?"

"What is the citizenship of parents, spouse, or other relatives?"

Requirement that applicant furnish naturalization papers or alien card prior to employment.

SUBJECT: **NATIONAL ORIGIN**

Acceptable: "Are you fluent in any languages other than English?" (You may ask this question only if it relates to the job for which the applicant is applying.)

Discriminatory: Questions as to lineage, ancestry, national origin, nationality, descent or parentage of applicant, applicant's parents or spouse.

"What is your mother tongue? What language do you commonly use?"

"Dombrowski...that's Polish, isn't it?"

"How did you acquire the ability to speak a foreign language?"

SUBJECT: **SEX, MARITAL STATUS, FAMILY**

Acceptable: Name and address of parent or guardian if applicant is a minor.

Statement of company policy regarding work assignment of employees who are related.

Discriminatory: "Are you male or female?"

Questions that indicate marital status.

"Is that Miss or Mrs.?"

"Are you married?"

"What does your husband think about you working outside the home?"

"Are you living with your spouse?"

"Do you live with your parents?"

SUBJECT: **RACE, COLOR**

Acceptable: None.

Discriminatory: "What is your race?"

Any questions regarding applicant's race, color, complexion, color of hair, eyes, or skin.

SUBJECT: **PHYSICAL DESCRIPTION, PHOTOGRAPH**

Acceptable: Statement that a photograph of the person may be taken after employment.

Discriminatory: Questions about an applicant's height and weight in the pre-employment interview.

Request that an applicant affix a photograph to the application.

Request a photo after interview but before employment.

SUBJECT: **PHYSICAL CONDITION, DISABILITY**

Acceptable: "Are you able to perform the essential job functions of this job with or without reasonable accommodation?"

Discriminatory: Questions regarding applicant's general medical condition, state of health or illnesses in the pre-employment interview.

Questions regarding receipt of Worker's Compensation.

SUBJECT: **RELIGION**

Acceptable: Statement by employer of regular days, hours or shifts to be worked and the expectations of regular attendance.

Discriminatory: "What is your religion?"

"What church do you attend?"

"What are your religious holidays?"

SUBJECT: **ARREST OR CONVICTIONS OF A CRIME**

Acceptable: "Have you ever been convicted of a felony?" (Such a question must be accompanied by a statement that a conviction will not necessarily disqualify applicant from employment.)

Discriminatory: "Have you ever been arrested?"

SUBJECT:	**BONDING**
Acceptable:	Statement that bonding is a condition of hire.
Discriminatory:	Question regarding refusal or cancellation of bonding.
SUBJECT:	**MILITARY SERVICE**
Acceptable:	Questions regarding relevant skills acquired during applicant's U.S. Military service.
Discriminatory:	General questions regarding military service such as date and type of discharge. Questions regarding service in a foreign military.
SUBJECT:	**ECONOMIC STATUS**
Acceptable:	None.
Discriminatory:	Questions regarding applicant's current or past assets, liabilities or credit rating including bankruptcy or garnishment.
SUBJECT:	**ORGANIZATIONS, ACTIVITIES**
Acceptable:	"Please tell me about job-related organizations, clubs, professional societies, or other associations to which you belong. You may omit those that indicate your race, religious creed, color, national origin, ancestry, sex, or age."
Discriminatory:	"Please tell me about all organizations, clubs, societies and lodges to which you belong."
SUBJECT:	**CHILD CARE**
Acceptable:	"Do you know any reason why you might not be able to come to work on time every day?" (Acceptable only if the question is asked of every applicant, regardless of sex.)
Discriminatory:	"How many children do you have?" "Who takes care of your children while you are working?" "How old are your children?" "Do you plan to have children?"
SUBJECT:	**REFERENCES**
Acceptable:	"By whom were you referred for a position here?" "Name persons willing to provide professional and/or character references for you."
Discriminatory:	Questions of applicant's former employers or acquaintances that elicit information specifying the applicant's race, color, religion, creed, national origin, ancestry, sex, age, physical handicap or disability, medical condition, or marital status.
SUBJECT:	**IN CASE OF EMERGENCY**
Acceptable:	Name and address of person to be notified in case of accident or emergency.
Discriminatory:	Name and address of relative to be notified in case of accident or emergency.

APPENDIX C

Major Federal Laws and Regulations Affecting Personnel Management

Space limitations only permit mention of the most important features of these laws. Consult professional advice before acting on this information.

LAW OR REGULATION	COVERAGE	BRIEF SUMMARY	ENFORCEMENT AGENCY
Fair Labor Standards Act (FLSA), 1938	Generally, employers with two employees handling goods moving in interstate commerce and annual dollar volume sales of $500,000; certain types of employers have lower or no dollar volume thresholds.	Minimum wage of $4.25/hr. overtime pay after 40 hours/week at time and 1/2 regular rate and accurate time records required for all non-exempt employees. Child labor restrictions.	U.S. Dept. of Labor, Wage Hour Division
(Walsh-Healey) Public Contracts Act, 1936	Employees of employers with fed. gov't supply contracts in excess of $10,000 who work on gov't contract.	Employer must pay covered employees time and 1/2 after 40 hours in a week.	U.S. Dept. of Labor, Wage Hour Division
McNamara-O'Hara Service Contract Act (MOSCA)	Employers with federal gov't service contracts in excess of $2,500 involving use of service employees.	Employer must pay specified minimum hourly rates and specified fringe benefits.	U.S. Dept. of Labor, Wage Hour Division

233

LAW OR REGULATION	COVERAGE	BRIEF SUMMARY	ENFORCEMENT AGENCY
Davis-Bacon Act, 1931	Federal public works contractor on contracts in excess of $2,000.	Employer must pay specified minimum hourly rates and specified fringe benefits.	Contracting agency and/or U.S. Dept. of Labor's Wage Hour Division
Migrant and Seasonal Agricultural Worker Protection Act (MSPA)	Most agricultural employers including forestry operations; farm labor contractors.	Requires disclosure of job terms, record-keeping, payment of wages when due, housing and vehicle safety standards for migrant and seasonal workers; contractor licensing.	U.S. Dept. of Labor
Contract Work Hours and Safety Standards Act (CWHSSA)	Federal contracts including construction requiring employment of laborers and mechanics.	Employer must pay one and 1/2 times basic rate for hours over 40 in a week.	U.S. Dept. of Labor
Family and Medical Leave Act (FMLA), 1993	Employers engaged in interstate commerce with 50+ employees.	Employer must provide eligible employees with up to 12 weeks of unpaid, job-protected leave annually for certain family and medical reasons	U.S. Dept. of Labor, Wage Hour Division
Title VII of the Civil Rights Act of 1964	Employers engaged in interstate commerce with 15+ employees.	Prohibits discrimination because of race, color, national origin, religion, sex, pregnancy (including childbirth or related condition).	Equal Employment Opportunity Commission
Title I of the Americans with Disabilities Act of 1990	Employers engaged in interstate commerce with 25+ employees (7/26/92). Employers engaged in interstate commerce with 15+ employees (7/26/94).	Prohibits dscrimination in terms, conditions, and privileges of employment against individuals with disabilities who, with or without reasonable accommodation, can perform essential functions of job.	Equal Employment Opportunity Commission

LAW OR REGULATION	COVERAGE	BRIEF SUMMARY	ENFORCEMENT AGENCY
Section 1981, Title 42 U.S.C. (Civil Rights Act of 1866)	All private employers, including individuals regardless of size or dollar volume.	Prohibits racial and ethnic bias in employment.	Private lawsuits
Executive Order 11246, 1965	Employers with government contracts in excess of $10,000 in any 12 month period.	Requires anti-discrimination clause in contract plus written affirmative action plan for single contract of $50,000+ and 50+ employees.	U.S. Dept. of Labor's Office of Federal Contract Compliance Programs
Age Discrimination in Employment Act, 1967, (ADEA) including Older Workers Benefit Protection Act (OWBPA), 1990	Employers engaged in interstate commerce with 20+ employees.	Prohibits age discrimination in employment, including benefits, for employees age 40 or over.	Equal Employment Opportunity Commission
Equal Pay Act of 1963 (EPA)	Generally, employers with two employees handling goods moving in interstate commerce and annual dollar volume sales of $500,000; certain types of employers have lower or no dollar volume thresholds. (Same as Fair Labor Standards Act.)	Prohibits pay differentials on basis of sex in substantially equal work requiring equal skill, effort and responsibility under similar working conditions. No exemption for executive, administrative, professional, and outside sales employees.	Equal Employment Opportunity Commission
Rehabilitation Act of 1973, Section 503	Employers with government contracts in excess of $10,000.	Requires affirmative action and non-discrimination in employment of handicapped persons. Written AAP required if 50+ employees and contract of $50,000+	U.S. Dept. of Labor's Office of Federal Contract Compliance Programs
Rehabilitation Act of 1973, Section 504	Employers with government contracts in excess of $10,000	No discrimination against, denying benefits to, or exclusion from participation, including employment, by any	Federal Agency responsible for providing financial assistance

LAW OR REGULATION	COVERAGE	BRIEF SUMMARY	ENFORCEMENT AGENCY
		qualified handicapped individual.	
Employee Polygraph Protection Act of 1988 (EPPA)	Employers subject to the FLSA. Exemptions for governments, certain government contractors, and employers in the security and drug industries.	Generally prohibits the use of "lie detectors" and lie detector results in private employment. Limited exemptions apply for certain internal investigations.	U.S. Dept. of Labor
Federal Military Selective Service Act	Employers in interstate commerce.	Gives employee returning from U.S. Military service the same wages, benefits, and rights as the employee would have received had he/she not left. Discrimination against Reservists barred.	U.S. Dept. of Labor, Veterans' Employment Service
Vietnam Era Veteran Readjustment Assistance Act, 1974	Employers with government contract of $10,000 or more.	Requires affirmative action regarding Vietnam era veterans and disabled veterans. Written AAP required if 50+ employees and a contract of $50,000+.	U.S. Dept. of Labor's Office of Federal Contract Compliance Programs
Immigration Reform and Control Act of 1986 (IRCA)	All employers.	Prohibits hiring of illegal aliens. Requires verification and record-keeping of work authorization documents.	U.S. Dept. of Justice, Immigration and Naturalization Service
Drug-Free Workplace Act of 1988	Employers with federal contracts of $25,000 or more; all federal grant recipients.	Establish drug-free awareness program and make good faith effort to carry out; requires penalties or rehabilitation for employees convicted of workplace drug offenses.	Federal agency that contracts or provides assistance

LAW OR REGULATION	COVERAGE	BRIEF SUMMARY	ENFORCEMENT AGENCY
Department of Transportation Drug Testing Regulations	All employers operating vehicles over 26,000 pounds, buses over 15 people, or moving hazardous materials; other regulation sections cover aviation, railroad, shipping, and natural gas industries.	Requires employers to conduct drug tests of certain employees in compliance with strict regulations, provide education and minimal Employee Assistance Programs (EAP's).	Federal Highway Administration, U.S. Coast Guard, FAA, Federal Railroad Administration, Urban Mass Transportation Administration
Worker Adjustment and Retaining Notification Act (WARN), 1988	Employers with at least 100 employees.	With some exceptions, requires 60-day notice to employees and state and local governments before layoffs of 50 or more employees.	DOL issues regulations, but WARN is enforced only by private lawsuit.
Social Security Act (FICA), 1935	Employers who pay over $50 per quarter in wages	Employer and employee each must contribute 7.65% of wages up to $55,500 and 1.45% on excess up to $130,200 for 1992. Withholding required. Wage base subject to annual adjustment.	U.S. Social Security Administration and Internal Revenue Service
Federal Unemployment Tax Act (FUTA), 1935	Employers who employ one or more persons 20 or more weeks/year.	Must contribute 0.8% (varies with credits for participation in state unemployment programs) up to $7,000 of each employee's wages.	Internal Revenue Service
Employee Retirement Income Security Act of 1974 (ERISA)	Employers in interstate commerce.	Requires extensive pension and welfare plan reporting, plus disclosure to participants and beneficiaries; minimum participation vesting and funding standards for pension plans, including	U.S. Dept. of Labor, Office of Pension and Welfare Benefits and Pension Benefit Guaranty Corporation

LAW OR REGULATION	COVERAGE	BRIEF SUMMARY	ENFORCEMENT AGENCY
		profit-sharing plans; plan termination insurance for pension plans.	
Consolidated Omnibus Budget Reconciliation Act of 1985 (COBRA)	Employers in interstate commerce and who claim tax deduction for group health plan expenses or who have "highly compensated employees" participating in group health plans; exception if under 20 employees in preceeding year.	Requires provision of continuation coverage under employer's group health plan to employees, spouses and/or dependent children upon the occurrence of specified events, including termination of employment or reduction in hours.	U.S. Dept. of Labor and Internal Revenue Service
Health Maintenance Organization Act (HMO), 1973	Employers subject to the FLSA's minimum wage provision with 25+ employees, offering a health benefits plan, and with at least 25 employees in HMO service area.	Employer must offer membership in a qualified HMO if available where employees live. Voluntarily or upon demand by qualified HMO.	U.S. Dept. of Health & Human Services' Office of Health Maintenance Organization
National Labor Relations Act (NLRA), (Wagner Act), 1935	Employers in interstate commerce.	Employee rights to engage in protected concerted activity and organize or decertify union.	National Labor Relations Board
Railway Labor Act	Airlines, railroads, express co's., some related co's.	Regulates co.-union elections/mandatory dispute-resolution processes.	Attorney General or private federal court suits.
Occupational Safety and Health Act (OSHA), (Williams-Steiger), 1970	Employers in interstate commerce.	Employer must furnish safe employment according to designated workplace standards; record-keeping; no retaliation against employees for exercising rights.	OSHA, U.S. Dept. of Labor

LAW OR REGULATION	COVERAGE	BRIEF SUMMARY	ENFORCEMENT AGENCY
Consumer Credit Protection Act. Title III (Federal Wage Garnishment Law)	Employers under the federal Wage & Hour Law.	Restricts garnishment withholding to 25% or less of disposable income. Allows larger deductions for support/alimony garnishments. No discharge for one or more garnishments of one debt.	U.S. Dept. of Labor's Wage & Hour Division
Fair Credit Reporting Act, 1970	Employers in interstate commerce.	Disclosure to applicants/employees intent to use investigative consumer report and, on request, nature/scope of investigation. Must inform applicant/employee if credit report is related to adverse action and disclose credit agency.	Federal Trade Commission

SUGGESTED READINGS

Atkinson, Lynn. *State and Federal EEO Compliance Encyclopedia.* Business & Legal Reports, Inc., 1995.

Bell, Howard H. *The Complete Guide to Interviewing: How to Hire the Best.* Homewood, IL: Dow Jones-Irwin, 1989.

Brounstein, Marty and Ron Visconti. *Effective Recruiting Strategies—A Practical Guide for Success.* Los Altos, CA: Crisp Publications, 1992.

Carr, Clay. *The New Manager's Survival Manual.* New York, NY: John Wiley & Sons, 1995.

Castagnera, James O. Esq. *Employment Law Answer Book* 2nd ed. New York, NY: Panel Publishers, 1993.

Cook, Mary F., ed. *The Human Resources Yearbook.* Englewood Cliffs, NJ: Prentice Hall, 1995.

Dube, Lawrence E. Jr. *The Hiring Handbook.* Greenvale, NY: Panel Publishers, 1990.

Fear, Richard A. and Robert J. Chiron. *The Evaluation Interview.* New York, NY: McGraw-Hill, 1990.

Fitz-enz, Jac. *How to Measure Human Resources Management.* New York, NY: McGraw-Hill, 1995.

Hacker, Carol. *Hiring Top Performers—350 Great Interview Questions for People Who Need People.* Alpharetta, GA: 1994.

Holton, Bill and Cher. *The Manager's Short Course—A Complete Course in Leadership Skills for the First-Time Manager.* New York, NY: John Wiley & Sons, 1992.

Levesque, Joseph, D. *The Human Resource Problem-Solvers Handbook.* New York, NY: Prentice Hall, 1991.

Ludlow, Ron and Fergus Panton. *The Essence of Successful Staff Selection.* Englewood Cliffs, NJ: Prentice Hall International, 1991.

Marsh, Peter. *Eye to Eye-How People React.* Topsfield, MA: Salem House Publishers, 1988.

McGill, Ann, M. *Hiring the Best.* Homewood, IL: Business One Irwin/ Mirror Press, 1994.

McKenna, Eugene and Nic Beech. *The Essence of Human Resource Management.* Englewood Cliffs, NJ: Prentice Hall International, 1995.

Mercer, Michael W. *Hire the Best and Avoid the Rest.* New York, NY: AMACOM, 1993.

Pinsker, Richard J. *Hiring Winners-Profile, Interview, Evaluation—A 3-Step Process.* New York, NY: AMACOM, 1991.

Risser, Rita. *Stay Out of Court: The Manager's Guide to Preventing Employees Lawsuits.* Englewood Cliffs, NJ: Prentice Hall, 1995.

Robertson, Cliff. *Live Right, Fire Right—A Manager's Guide to Employment Practices That Avoid Lawsuits.* New York, NY: McGraw Hill, 1992.

Sack, Steven Mitchell. *From Hiring to Firing.* New York, NY: Legal Strategies Publications, 1995.

Steingold, Fred S. *The Employer's Legal Handbook.* Berkeley, CA: Nolo Press, 1994.

Swan, William S. *How to Pick the Right People Program.* New York, NY: John Wiley & Sons, 1989.

Weiss, Donald H. *Fair, Square & Legal Safe Hiring, Managing & Firing Practices to Keep You & Your Company Out of Court.* New York, NY: American Management Association, 1995.

Wendover, Robert W. *High Performance Hiring-Attracting & Retaining the Best.* Los Altos, CA.: Crisp Publications, 1991.

Wendover, Robert W. *Smart Hiring for Your Business.* Naperville, IL: Sourcebooks Trade, 1993.

Worthington, E.R. and Anita E. Worthington. *People Investment-How to Make Your Hiring Decisions Pay Off For Everyone.* Grants Pass, OR: Oasis Press, 1993.

Worthington, E.R. and Anita E. Worthington. *Staffing A Small Business: Hiring, Compensation and Evaluating.* Grants Pass, OR: Oasis Press, 1987.

Wright, Robert S. and Deborah George Wright. *Creating and Maintaining the Drug-Free Workforce.* New York, NY: McGraw-Hill, 1993.

INDEX